FIND *your* VOICE *in the* DARKNESS

Shine Your Light to Serve Your Soul Purpose

**Medium
Sky Raye**

©2021 by Medium Sky Raye

All rights reserved. No part of this book may be reproduced in whole or part, or stored in a retrieval system, or transmitted in any form or by any means, electronic, mechanical, photocopying, recording, or otherwise, without the written permission of the author.

ISBN: 978-1-7363289-0-3

Library of Congress Control Number: 2020925275

Printed in Loganton, Pennsylvania by Medium Sky Raye

This book is not intended for use as a source of physical or mental health, medical, or business advice. All readers are advised to seek the services of competent professionals in the physical or mental health, medical, and business fields.

The advice and strategies found within may not be suitable for every situation. This work is sold with the understanding that neither the author nor the publisher is held responsible for the results accrued from the advice in this book.

While all attempts have been made to verify information provided for this publication, the publisher assumes no responsibility for errors, omissions, or contrary interpretation of the subject matter herein. Any perceived slights of specific persons, peoples, or organizations are unintended.

For more information or for bulk orders, visit https://MediumSkyRaye.com.

Table of Contents

Dedication. v

Foreword vii

Acknowledgments. xi

Introduction xiii

A Special Bonus Gift from Sky xix

Part I Spiritual Awakening After Loss, Transformation, and Serving Your Higher Self 1

Chapter 1: The Bond That Never Breaks: Life After Death 3

Chapter 2: Self-Transformation After a Traumatic Loss 17

Chapter 3: Manifesting What You Desire 35

Chapter 4: Energy Work 47

Chapter 5: Working with Your Spirit Guides. 65

Part II   My Journey Through the Dark 79

Chapter 6: My Intuitive Journey 81

Chapter 7: A Haunting 87

Chapter 8: Where There Is Light, There Is
　　　　　 Also Dark. 101

Chapter 9: Where to Go from Here 123

Glossary. 129

About the Author 135

Dedication

This book is lovingly dedicated to…

The Creator of this beautiful universe. I am grateful beyond words for all that you have taught me and provided for me in this lifetime.

My father Anthony J. Caprio III. Thank you for being my hero and best friend. You have been my biggest supporter even after your death. I wouldn't be who I am without you. I love you.

My spirit guides and spirit team that pushed me through every obstacle, loss, or challenge in my life. Thank you for always supporting me during my lessons with patience and pure love. You were my hope and faith when I didn't have the strength to move through my life.

And all the beautiful souls whom I have had the privilege to meet during this lifetime who are now departed. I am honored to serve as your voice always. We are forever and I am deeply proud to be able to help others through your loving messages to loved ones. Thank you for trusting and believing in me and allowing me to serve as God's messenger.

Foreword

Sky Raye is just the person to write this book, *Find Your Voice in the Darkness: Shine Your Light to Serve Your Soul Purpose.* I know she will be a blessing to you as she is and has been for so many others. Get ready! She is a *spiritual powerhouse*, and, when she touches your life, you will see the possibilities available to you and the transformation that awaits you. She goes first, living her life as an example and leading the way.

Sky Raye is the guide to show you how to not just overcome but to *become* who you really are. In healing yourself, so much opens up to you, including manifesting what you desire. In the past few years, she has done exactly this, rising from her own ashes like the Phoenix over and over again to become the person she is today, living her truth and sharing her light. And she is magnetic!

People who encounter the energy that is Sky find themselves catalyzed to stretch and grow. She will never ask you to do what she hasn't already done many times. Her life is a testament to the rewards that await you when you are willing to do this.

It's all energy, and this is part of what she is here to share with you. Life after death is the bond that never breaks, and she communicates with those who have gone to the other side for those who are here. Manifesting what you desire is all about your own energy, and she shows you how it's done. Sky also works with her spirit guides and yours to help you understand these powerful energies available to you and how they can support you in your life, your growth, and your healing. She is very tapped into her intuition and will share with you how important it is to learn how to work with this part of you for your highest and best good.

Sky Raye understands all too well the balance of the energies of what we know as Light and Dark, and she is able to navigate both for the benefit of those she helps every day. She is a sought-after expert in the paranormal world and helps make sense of the things that have been such a mystery for so many, bringing her own unique perspective and flair to her work in this realm.

Sky has had several darkest hours she readily shares with her readers, her community, her clients, and her students in hopes that, by sharing her journey and her story and speaking her truth, she will help you to find and live yours.

Above all else, Sky wants to help you understand that all these aspects of you and your world are available to you right now. They co-exist within you and around you, and it is up to you to take this journey of hope and faith and emerge in your truth and your light.

Read the book, connect with Sky online, and discover a spiritual teacher whose time is now. Guess who else's time is now? Yours.

Michelle Barr
Coach, Intuitive Strategist, Healer, Mindset Mentor, Author and Spiritual Business Expert
www.MichelleBarr.com

Acknowledgments

I wish to acknowledge my family, friends, colleagues, and my personal business coach for all the love and support to help make this book happen.

I want to thank my editor, Diana Henderson, and my publishing and marketing strategist, Diana M. Needham, for helping my vision come to life and making this book a reality.

Thank you to my clients for all the love and support you offered and for being patient with me while this book creation process took place.

I extend a big thank you to Celebrity Medium Thomas John for everything you taught me along the way.

To my coach, Michelle Barr, you have been with me since the beginning. Thank you immensely for your inspiration and encouragement.

I am beyond blessed to have connected with such amazing spiritual entrepreneurs that helped pave my way.

Introduction

"Are you the only one here with Anthony?" the doctor asked as he approached me, flanked by six nurses.

Taking note of the concern on their faces, my stomach knotted up, my eyes uncontrollably filled with tears, and my knees trembled as I viscerally sensed the news they were about to deliver was more dire than I ever imagined.

"The cancer has spread in two places in your dad's colon. I have never seen such an advanced case with his reports of so few symptoms. He is in stage four."

Suddenly I was in the worst nightmare I could ever imagine. I totally lost it. How could this be happening? Dad never got sick and he never missed work. He was only 64! He was my hero, my best friend, my superman. I thought I would have him in my life for a very long time.

Having come in with my dad for what we assumed was a routine procedure to rule out any issues, I was totally unprepared for what the doctor was saying.

"Stop crying!" the nurse barks at me. "You have to be strong for him and not show your pain. Your father is in the recovery room waking up, and we have to go in and tell him this news."

I couldn't believe I was being told what to feel in that moment. As the shock set in and without time to process this news, I wanted to scream. I felt like I would pass out.

I had to go face my dad with these strangers to tell him he had cancer and it was not looking good. I did not know how to feel or what to say to him.

Dad was happy to see me, talking like everything was okay. I stared at him and thought, *This cannot be happening!* I heard the nurse's voice again in my head, commanding, *"Do not cry!"*

As I stood there, I was in denial that this was happening. Sadness, anxiety, and fear rose up within me. My struggle with depression and thoughts of suicide flooded my soul yet again.

Everything in my life was about to change forever. After the doctor and nurses left the room, Dad explained that he knew he could have prevented this if he had been more proactive and had followed up with his first examination after the death of his father, my grandfather. Grandfather also had cancer at age 86. He'd died of heart failure 10 years prior to the very day my dad was diagnosed. In those moments after he received the news, I realized I was watching him come to terms with his illness and witnessing firsthand his grief about the situation. As he talked about his own grief, I realized I would have to deal with my own.

Thus began the next leg of my journey as a healer, professional psychic, and medium.

Often, grief and trauma leave us feeling rudderless—lost at sea—unable to move forward because we become stuck in the pain. Sadly, many times it takes a traumatic loss and deep grief to wake us up to what we have been blind to in the past.

I know that place all too well. My life has been filled with difficulties and loss. Any genuine spirit medium and psychic would likely tell you the same. Part of our journey is to experience the human condition and learn ways to rise above life's pain and sorrow in order to help others find their way onto the path of healing.

Are you on your own spiritual path and dealing with the deep grief of losing something or someone dear to you?

Are you longing for connection and a deeper understanding of the spiritual realm so you can find the answers, clarity, and peace your soul so desperately seeks?

Are you looking for validation of what you have experienced in life so you can find peace and alignment with your spiritual gifts and what you are called to do?

If you feel abandoned in the midst of a sea of darkness, know that you are not alone, and this book is for you.

Whatever issues you are encountering, a way exists to move past them, to evolve and rise beyond them.

Through my own story and the stories of others in this book, my hope is that you will find the path to a better life, free of the shadow that may seem to engulf the world or your own life. Know that, together with the light of your spirit, you can do anything.

We *can* progress beyond the pain. Whatever challenges or losses we endure in life will eventually become our greatest teachers. They may even hold the keys to deep healing for self, and, when we're ready to integrate the wisdom we gather from those experiences, we may share those gifts we've gained with others who walk a similar path.

Inside this book, you'll discover how to:

- Overcome losses, grief, and obstacles, and find hope when you may not want to go on living
- Let go of wounds from the past and move forward to accomplish your mission
- Uncover your purpose and embrace your mission as you follow your heart, listen to your spirit, and walk your own unique path
- Release negative energy and thoughts, and find alignment with who you truly are
- Use energy work as a powerful tool for healing
- Work with your own spirit guides who are here to guide you on your journey

Later in the book, I share my own story of love, loss, light, and shadow. I would never wish on anyone the journey I have walked. You'll witness how I faced demons and experienced death itself to find my own path to wholeness and peace again.

Let's begin.

A Special Bonus Gift from Sky

Now that you have your copy of ***Find Your Voice in the Darkness: Shine Your Light to Serve Your Soul Purpose***, you are on your way to finding your true purpose that aligns your deepest desires and knowing how to manifest your vision and navigate your way forward, despite the darkness, grief, or pain you may have experienced before now.

Inside this book you will discover how to return to yourself again and restore the peace, hope, and faith that you may have lost along the way. These are the things that will propel you forward.

In order to help you along the journey, I've created a special bonus gift just for you as a reader of this book. It's a ***Spiritual Journey Meditation*** kit, a series of three audio meditations to help you

- Reduce anxiety and connect with your natural state of being.
- Connect with your loved ones, spirit guides, and angels who help you during your journey.
- Explore how to ground yourself, clear your energy and recharge to open your natural gifts to serve your soul purpose

Just go to www.MediumSkyRaye.com/freegift and tell me where to send it.

The sooner you know how to align with your soul and seek to live according to the wisdom of your higher self, the faster you can bring miracles into this world and create the life you've envisioned.

I'm in your corner. Let me know if I can help further.

Here's to your healing, peace, joy, and aligned purpose!

Best,
Sky Raye

PART I

Spiritual Awakening After Loss, Transformation and Serving Your Higher Self

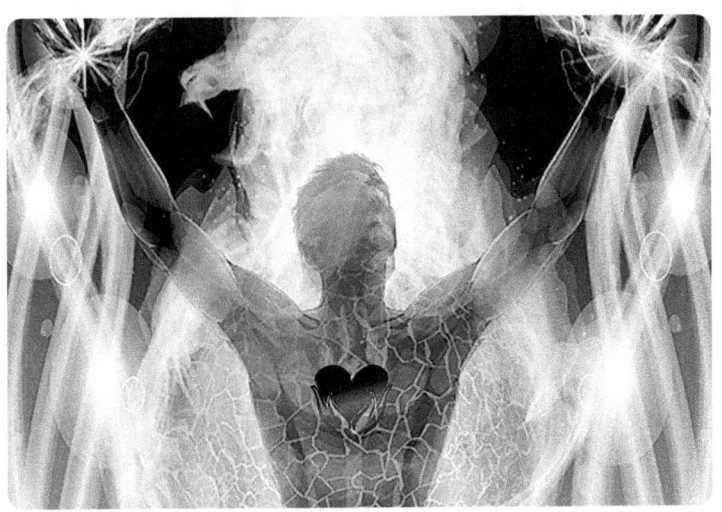

CHAPTER ONE

The Bond That Never Breaks: Life After Death

We are more than our physical form. We are mind, body, and soul, but our essence is the soul or the etheric body, our connection to all things. Once we leave this physical shell or shed our bodies when we die, our soul still exists.

The easiest way to explain it is that we are spiritual beings in a physical body having a human experience. My loved ones who have passed came to me and told me, "I am not in pain; I am so happy and at peace." Believe it or not, they hang around us because we are the ones not doing so well after they leave. Since I have lost many close family members and friends, I have seen this on several occasions.

Grief looks different for everyone. There are many stages to grief, and there is no right way or wrong way to mourn a loss. It is an intensely personal and individual journey. Some of us take longer than others to process a loved one's passing, and that is okay.

We do not need to ask permission to grieve. Just do it in your own way without any expectation of how it will unfold or how long it will last. We all need to embrace healing by going through our own process, allowing time to understand how to move on and find out who we are again after a major change like a traumatic loss or death.

Through the mourning process, we rediscover who we are and what our purpose is. This is a gift that our loved ones want us to be aware of. They did not go away because they wanted to leave us or make us hurt. They left knowing that we would have an opportunity to make the best out of our own lives. Life is a gift, and it is short. We often do not know when we will say our last words or kiss and hug them for the last time. Through our losses, we learn to appreciate life on a much deeper level.

When a tragedy happens, we are eventually forced to awaken. That is heartbreak's gift to us. Of course, I certainly didn't always see it that way. I struggled with suicidal thoughts and depression after the loss of my dad, who was my best friend. Around the same time he was going through his cancer treatments and surgeries, I also was experiencing some major health issues. I was in denial about the situation, and I honestly did not believe he wouldn't make it. My faith was always with me throughout this journey.

A Priceless Bond and Heartwarming Validations

In the beginning of March 2020, I took an online spiritual entrepreneur business class and was introduced to so many talented people—CEOs and self-made individuals with spiritual businesses who have so much to offer with their leadership skills and gifts. I was amazed to have connected with these people who were all networking as I was. We were offered a private group in which to chat and connect during several weeks of training. It was a great experience for me.

I offered free psychic and mediumship email readings within the group. As I was going through my emails to respond to all of them, one stood out to me. It was from an angelic woman in the group named K.C. She asked for a one-question reading. I looked at her message and decided to reply in hopes she would set up a Zoom session with me.

As a clairaudient (someone who can hear sounds that are beyond the reach of ordinary experience or capacity), I sometimes receive auditory messages. I was told by a young soul that she needed a healing message. I did not hesitate and contacted her straight away to schedule a time and date for her reading.

When we got on Zoom, we met and talked for a few minutes, and I started receiving information clairvoyantly (visually). I instantly began to view images. A download of memories is the only way to describe it. I saw off-roading in a black truck and just having fun. I observed the color green and knew that it was important, and yet I was not sure what it represented. Then I experienced an overwhelming feeling of sadness. I felt depressed and despondent.

A young male started speaking to me about school and how he had a hard time, experiencing difficulty from having been bullied . I realized this was a young man, not yet an adult. My heart was breaking as this boy connecting with me said, "I am sorry, Mom. I am so sorry."

This was K.C.'s son. As a tear rolled down my cheek, I tried to stay focused on my healing work and not let my emotions overtake me. I heard him repeat for the third time how he was sorry, and he said, "I love you." He said he was responsible for his death and was deeply regretful about what had happened.

Another of my gifts is clairsentience, which means I can feel someone else's pain in my own body. Here, I felt pain in my head and an instant impact. I heard him say he was responsible for taking his own life.

As the reading went on, her son took me back to a shared memory that K.C. experienced a few months prior. I started talking and felt as if I left my body. I took a deep breath and released it and then shared with K.C. what I was seeing. I told her that her son was showing me something. He took me to another place, a different dimension, where I saw the silhouette of a male energy. He was a bright light, a soul being. I kept describing what I saw and how I felt during this memory or experience, and then I heard him say, "I will walk with you now."

I could not believe what I was seeing: There were two spirit beings embracing one another in this light, and they connected as one. I heard him say, "I love you, but you need to go back. You need to do your work and help heal people. I love you and I will always be with you."

This was truly amazing. I could hardly believe what I was being shown. Their souls met together on the other side and joined as one. I saw him step away, and I felt her come back into her body. I took another deep breath.

I just witnessed a bond that could never be severed even after death. We have a soul, and that soul is forever. The bond between a mother and child is the ultimate relationship of unconditional love.

K.C. was able to validate all the information that came through for her. She said that her son had identified himself as an old soul while he was living and explained that he did have a hard life even at 17. In order to validate that this was her son during the reading, he shared all the things he liked and did not like during his short life.

She confirmed that the shared memory of oneness stemmed from her own near-death experience. She had gone in for knee surgery and flatlined on the operating table. The vision I received was her exact experience while she flatlined.

I was awestruck at the end of her mediumship reading and thankful for her validations. Spirit astonishes me every time I connect. I knew what I was feeling from spirit, but I was in shock myself that spirit could connect me on such a deep level. I understood what I was seeing and relayed the encounter exactly as I received it.

Seeing the Bigger Picture

This story has inspired me, and I hope that, if you have experienced the loss of a child or a loved one, you can now understand how strong that bond of love is. It's eternal. My work has taught me that the only thing we take with us when we die is the love we have for one another.

I have to say the hardest thing for me personally is encountering children in spirit. I am a mother and have had my own experiences with anxiety, depression, and suicide with my child. I also have struggled personally with these issues. This was something that I knew far too well. I could understand and feel true compassion. I was able to relay this information clearly because spirit uses our own experiences to help mediums get clear messages.

The most precious gift a mother could ever receive is to bring life to another being and understand what unconditional love means. The bonds between a mother and child can never be broken, not even after death. We can have a better understanding of how strong a connection it is, and, with faith, we can learn to adapt and be resilient after the loss of a child.

K.C. expressed that her son's tragic death had provided a gift, a blessing in disguise. What I can say is that she found herself again and discovered her soul purpose as a result of this devastating loss. This is now her strength; this is her story and her truth. She told me she is truly blessed and understands the bigger picture, and, with her faith and love, she has been able to move into a space of peace and acceptance.

I hope that this story will help others heal. We all process grief so differently. I understand how difficult the journey is after such a loss. Until we have worked through our grief and healed enough, we cannot imagine why these things have happened or hope to comprehend them.

Healing Self to Help Others

Mediums must first heal themselves before they can help others. Most credible mediums have had hard lives, experienced horrible traumas, and have gone through a ton of health problems. We sacrifice a lot and have had to pay healers, counselors, coaches—you name it—to work through our issues. We have to come through our own shit, so to speak, to help heal others.

When we begin to heal ourselves first, then the journey of assisting others begins. Please do not be scared or feel ashamed to reach out for help! We all need support. The first step toward healing is reaching out.

We do not always recognize or understand how to get through grief. We are not meant to do this alone. Assistance and support are always available to us. Sometimes we have to seek the services of a few different types of traditional or nontraditional healers to get us through the process, but it's vital that we never give up. We have these experiences for a reason. We are meant to learn from them by figuring out a different way to cope and discovering how to become more resilient. This is a journey of understanding the self and continuously evolving.

I want you to know that we are all able to connect intuitively on some level. Our personal experiences make us unique and direct us in healing work. Most of us have had profound losses, perhaps even NDEs (near death experiences), along with trials and tribulations. Experiencing a great loss can completely change your life forever.

Grief: A Personal Journey

You may be familiar with the five stages of grief first proposed by Elisabeth Kübler-Ross in 1969: denial, anger, bargaining, depression, acceptance. We all experience those stages differently. We may skip a few and get stuck on one stage for months or years. We go through our own personal journey.

Grief, as we know, is an overpowering emotion and an intense process with no limits. I say this with great understanding because this is the place where I was stuck for several years. We can never prepare for this journey. It presents many challenges, obstacles, and difficulties.

It's no wonder the most common first stage is denial. We naturally try to protect ourselves during a time of loss to try and make sense of the situation. Human nature is fight or flight, and our natural response is to defend ourselves even from our sorrow when we do not know how to process it. During this stage we use denial to merely process our acceptance in our own time so we can figure out how to cope. Since my dad had the same job for over thirty years and never missed work, I was in denial about his illness. It is hard to imagine what life will look like without that special person you always believed would be there.

We are creatures of habit. Even if we get the opportunity to prepare as I did for my dad's last days, it still does not make things any easier. You just never know when you will see someone for the last time.

We need to be more grateful for what we have and not get complacent. None of us is perfect, and I admit I have taken a lot for granted at times. Since my dad died, I've tried to be more mindful and to appreciate what I have. I try to love and be the best I can be, but I certainly am not perfect. I need to be honest and be okay with being perfectly imperfect!

As I have seen in my own life and from clients' stories, this is often where guilt comes in. Even if we have the opportunity to prepare ourselves for loss, we still end up being hard on ourselves and often do not acknowledge that we have done our best. The most difficult part of such a journey is accepting the fact that we have no control over what happens. We just eventually learn to cope, realizing there is nothing we can do to alter the course of our loved ones' lives or prevent their deaths. Looking back, we may see there was a lesson for us to learn in this experience, perhaps blessings in disguise we couldn't fathom at the time.

My Story

I work closely with spirit, and those on the other side have taught me about the different ways we choose to leave this life. Even after doing a great deal of healing work and having countless encounters as a medium with those who have crossed over, I still had to face the challenges of grief and loss. I struggled with my faith and repeatedly asked why. I could not come to terms with knowing the biggest part of my life was missing. I wanted to be sure that nothing was left unsaid, to make the best of the last memories we could create together, and be supportive of my father in his final days.

I thought I did everything right. I was strong and I prepared as much as anyone could. What a bunch of crap! I was so wrong. I had no idea what I was about to go through. I became numb and angry. I hated the whole world and felt like I was target, like I had been ripped off. This was how I felt.

I had my faith and I wanted to be strong for my father and my family. I denied myself peace and personal time to try to process all the issues I was facing. I did not allow time to work on myself to stay healthy or to cope. My normal day-to-day vanished, and I lost hope, peace, trust, and most of all my faith. I was like a robot that was totally burned out.

From late October 2015 until March 2019, my life was hell. The world I had known prior to my father's death was just a memory. Everything I cherished was torn from me in multiple ways. I held it together for the three years prior, not knowing I was a ticking time bomb about to blow. I was weak and I was broken.

Because I was on such a spiritual path and already had a deeper understanding than many, I thought I should be able to heal myself. How wrong I was! When I finally realized that I needed the help of others who knew more than I did and accepted their wisdom and help, I found deeper healing.

I suggest that you find what you are called to try, and, if you are not getting the results you're looking for, search for other resources. Sometimes one way is not enough. I have seen traditional counselors my whole life, and I came to realize that I needed more than just being able to communicate how I felt.

If these words are resonating, you are in the right place. I have experienced so many ordeals in my life and found hope after battling trauma, depression, loss, grief, and after struggling with health issues. I have finally healed from my past traumas, which has prepared me to work in the way that I can best serve my clients with the healing services I now offer. This book is based on the wisdom and experience I have gained over time and offers you a chance to heal, clear, and move into a positive mindset, leaving limiting beliefs behind.

Embracing the Lessons

As you continue to read this book, I invite you to remember who you are and what your purpose is. My hope and prayer is that you will find your passion in life to carry on so you can do what makes you happy. You can't follow that path if, like I was, you are doing so much for others that you've forgotten what you truly want and what brings you joy and fulfillment.

In order to move past trauma and discover your true path, you may have to undergo a process of reprogramming. Beyond what you may have learned about letting go of limiting beliefs, don't be afraid to explore other ways to change how you think. When you stop limiting yourself to possibilities, true growth can happen. When we can give ourselves permission to fully receive, we can navigate our path more easily and embrace peace.

Please know that you are so important. Your story is important! It is your truth, your journey to finding your strength. We all are here for the human experience of learning, growing, and evolving as spiritual beings.

The loss of a loved one is devastating. The strong bonds and connections we all have differ in many ways. You cannot compare your personal loss to anyone else's. These connections are sacred. Know that your loved ones never leave you. They are forever loving, helping, and supporting you every day.

Our journey here is all about embracing the lessons we've come to learn so that we can progress and understand more about the human condition. Our loved ones in spirit are ceaselessly helping us on this journey.

CHAPTER TWO

Self-Transformation After a Traumatic Loss

Transformation, by its very nature, is dramatic change, a metamorphosis. After a traumatic loss, many seek a deeper spiritual or soul connection and to uncover what they truly desire in life. When life throws us a curveball that clearly isn't what we expected or hoped for, it is time to reevaluate.

Of course, we are creatures of habit. We like to be comfortable. As a result, we cling to those unhelpful behaviors that just do not get us anywhere. To move forward, we must genuinely want to change and be willing to do what it takes. The better we know ourselves, the more aligned our choices will be. Gaining your own self-awareness is an empowering, life-changing experience that increases feelings of self-worth and alleviates self-doubt.

Part of staying in our comfort zone is holding on to the old behaviors that led us to where we are now. In order to break out of that pattern, we must genuinely want our lives to be different and be willing to do what it takes to make that happen.

The first step is defining what we truly want. Most of us can quickly articulate what we *don't* want but have given no thought to what we *do* want. Once we are clear about our true desires, we can make decisions that move us closer to achieving them. Connecting to the feeling of what we envision for our future is the secret to creating what we want.

Thoughts are energy! If you get nothing else from this book, let that sink in. What we think about, the tapes that play and replay in our minds, whether good or bad, bring the results we see in our outer world. It is that simple: If you want your outer world to change, change how you think!

Whatever you envision and truly believe can be achieved. My fifth-grade teacher, an incredibly wise older gentleman, used affirmations and quotes to inspire and encourage all of us in his class. This is one that stayed with me, although I didn't fully understand it until much later in life. Just imagine: Whether good or bad, what we conceive, we will achieve!

Once we are self-aware and begin to live in the knowing that our thoughts are powerful, we can take inspired, aligned action to create the outcome we desire. No goal can be realized without actions, of course, and our goals need to be realistic and attainable. Take baby steps to start and make small, easily achieved changes first to boost your confidence.

When you are able to master the process of positive thinking and visualization, you can move on to something bigger. But setting small, reachable goals allows us to see proof of the changes that are happening, which is reason enough to keep going and creating more of everything we love.

When we reprogram with a positive mindset, we begin to shift our lives. Love and joy bring the highest vibration to energize our thoughts and visualizations. Make sure you are happy about what you are creating and bringing into your new world.

My own experience has taught me that connecting feelings such as love and joy with the thought of what I desire makes it become easier to manifest those aspirations. Remember to believe in yourself and be open to the idea that anything is possible. I am a living example of this philosophy and know firsthand how it works. This piece of the puzzle is so vital that I'll repeat this advice to help you fully understand it as we take this journey together.

Please be kind to yourself and allow yourself to accept and embrace the changes you make. Transforming your life starts with a new mindset. Become aware of bad habits, unhealthy patterns, and limiting beliefs. Once you are in control of the way you feel, you will begin to enjoy this new way of living. You will appreciate sensing things that are about to happen and relish seeing things fall into place, and you will adore witnessing the manifestations of your desires.

Here are the five process steps that will enable you to transform your life and create your dreams:

- Discover: Become consciously aware of familiar patterns, what you have been taught by conditioning to society's standards, limiting beliefs from growing up—all the things that make you feel *safe*. Explore conflicting beliefs that came from family dynamics.

- Shift: Look deeper for the root issue in the area of your life you want to change. Keep an eye out for situations and patterns that repeat. Be willing to make changes to energetically shift the outcome. You need to resolve the deeper issue and heal in order to serve your higher self.

- Act: To get a different result, you must change your actions. Setting powerful intentions creates a new energy in the now. Be present and follow through. If you feel fear as you make changes, that just means you are on your way to a new path. Be okay with being *uncomfortable*. Feeling safe is stagnate energy.

- Believe: We naturally act when we believe. Have faith in what you are worth and hold your new beliefs close to your heart. You have resolved

and healed to empower yourself. The universe responds to what we *feel*. You start to see evidence of your expected results by following through with the changes to your actions.
- Create: Create what you desire. When you are in alignment with your soul, you are tapping into your power. The universe clears a path to back you up as you take the steps to fully create your own reality and experiences.

How This Process Unfolded for Susan

In the early part of 2020, I started working with a client named Susan who sought help with her newly discovered spiritual path. She wanted to learn what she could do to advance on her life path.

I have to say that I love clients who want to evolve and move forward. When they get excited and become self-motivated, they invest in their transformation, and watching that shift is amazing.

Normally people come to me for a mediumship reading or other services before working one-on-one with me in coaching. She did not. Her path was different in every respect. I learn something new every day when working with spirit. I coached her first and then she scheduled a full reading.

Previously I had done a reading for this new client's daughter, which is how she found out about me and my business. Word of mouth travels fast, and I was so happy that she reached out to me. I work closely with my clients and hold a sacred space for them during our sessions. It is so important to make sure that my clients discover and identify their desires and needs in order to have a successful outcome.

When we defined and wrote out her short-term and long-term goals, she was ready to start doing her part. Notice I said she was *ready* to do her part. Not everyone has arrived at the level of readiness Susan displayed. I saw her *commit* to herself for the change of outcome she wanted to create. That doesn't mean she did not have to reevaluate, adjust, and course correct along the way. Even if we are unsure how we will get to our desired outcome, it's important to be flexible and willing to stay on track without knowing the how!

From the coaching I have received, I know that most people get to the action part and, because it does not happen in their expected time frame, they become frustrated and give up. It's vital to remain patient with yourself, to trust the process and your part in it, and believe that the way has already been made to bring your goal to fruition. Easier said than done, I know.

I was happy to observe Susan as she gave herself permission to love herself again. She offered herself the time to sit and write in her journal, which she had not done in years—time to reflect and be creative, time to come back to herself. I saw that she was beginning to remember all the things she once loved to do, and all the dreams she had were flooding her mind again! How amazing it was to listen to her passion and see her motivation gaining momentum as the days went by. I honestly had no clue that she would totally exceed her expectations as well as mine.

Her main goal was to focus on what she needed for herself. She wanted to have more energy, so we started her with a new health regimen. I had no idea that we would be planning her days and weeks accordingly.

Improving her health was what showed up for her, and she gave 100 percent to the effort. I was so proud of and inspired by her. Each client comes in for help at a different stage of grief and with varied expectations. As mentioned earlier, some of the stages we experience fully, some we skip, and some phases we do not go through at all.

Here are Susan's own words as she describes how she got back in touch with who she is.

> *When I first started sessions with my coach Sky, I was stuck in the same old routines, feeling bad about myself, fear, stress, anxiety, and low energy. I had a lack of willpower and the list goes on. Sky helped me to push my reset button and got me back on my path to clarity, unblocking the crap I was dealing with in life. I am*

connected to my higher self again and moving forward, freely loving myself and taking care of my health. I have clarity and think deeper once again.

Meditation has been key to connecting back to my true self and identity. I realize now to take the time for me in my quiet space so I can truly reflect to stay connected. I came up with a plan for myself with Sky's help. I am staying on course and focusing on writing, journaling, and staying resilient. My energy has shifted to a higher vibration, and now I have appreciation for the very air I breathe and my life.

The advice I want to give others is to not be afraid of change. My health is important to me, and I realize taking care of physical, mental, and spiritual health is key. Stay grounded, create the life you want, and rejoice in your own achievements.

Release Limiting Beliefs and Commit to Change

Investing in yourself by working on your self-love and self-worth is the most important step for anyone who is serious about changing. You will start to look for all the things that have been missing in your life from the inside, not the outside.

Seeking validation by looking outside ourselves and expecting others to make us happy never works. We are always left with disappointment when we expect others to take that role. That is not fair to anyone. I know this from experience. I had to stop playing the victim and own my shit! I needed to make myself accountable for my life, my own choices, and my inaction. For years I never realized that I was the one holding myself back from creating a happy life. That is my responsibility, no one else's.

I had a lot of healing work to do to get me to the point of being okay to decide what I wanted and why. What would make me happy? What did I want? I began to discover what made me happy. I thought about what that meant to me. I had to accept myself for who I really was.

This was the hardest part in my healing. I wanted to be accepted by my family and friends, but I did not accept myself. I was worried about what people would think of me, and I never gave myself credit for all the help and healing work that I had done with others. From a young age, we all have been programmed with limiting beliefs by our teachers, family, and friends. It's up to each of us to move beyond those constraints.

We often do not even realize these patterns and deeply ingrained ideas have kept us thinking small or left us feeling stuck. We question what is happening and why when we repeat these confining patterns. We try to figure out what has been going wrong. The answer is simple: We have been limiting who we are and what we are truly capable of achieving based on those programs created very early in life. We learn at a young age how to speak, what to believe, who to believe. We may even get baptized into a religion at birth because our family chooses to subscribe to that religion.

We all have the right to believe in whatever is comfortable for us. Each of us is unique, and it's okay to be different. We have to find our own identity and our own truth. When a situation arises that forces us to change and move out of the stagnant energy we have been stuck in, we start to shift into a new understanding. Usually this is caused by a traumatic experience or losing someone close to us.

Then we start to re-evaluate everything we might have thought we knew as truth. We explore our own beliefs about what is acceptable or right and realize someone else instilled their values in us. Society's standards also play a big part in this. If we live our lives according to someone else's vision or values, we aren't being our true, authentic self. In order to discover what and who we are, what we truly want, and our own beliefs and principles, we need to go deep within.

In order to make positive changes in life, we need to have a detailed plan. It doesn't have to be complicated. I try to simplify everything I teach into the easiest way to understand and work closely with my clients to create realistic and tangible goals to get instant results.

We can't do this work alone. Reprogramming your mindset can take time, but it can be rapid if you are willing to commit to yourself during the process. Invest in a coach to help with this practice. Research the leaders you are considering and make sure they have attained major goals themselves. Confirm that any mentor you choose is a mirror of what you want and aspire to be.

Linking Emotions to Intentions to Anchor Your Vision

The mind is the first tool in creating what you want. We visualize our desired outcome first. Consciously or unconsciously, we create positive or negative thoughts every second. The key is to *connect the why* to your goal. Why, you ask? To consciously create, you need to link emotion to the visualization of what you seek to bring into reality.

Let me give you an example of what I mean. I have an acquaintance whose deepest desire was to become a novelist. She had held this vision in her heart since she was a little girl, but she never really followed through with bringing this dream to reality. She had a number of limiting beliefs, ingrained by hard-working parents and by society, about the prospect of earning a living in the arts, so she found other occupations that were "steadier." Finally, when she reached a certain age and after losing her father, she felt an overwhelming yearning to write. But she had to dig deep inside to find her *why*. What emotion drove her passion for writing? She found the answer in joy, the pure elation she felt when making up stories and songs to entertain her family as a child, and the more profound joy that arose from the prospect of writing novels that shifted people's views and connected them more to their spirit. She finally realized her dream only after shifting beyond her limiting beliefs, bonding her intention to her why and the joy that lay behind it, and taking actions to bring her goal to fruition.

When you are deeply connected to why and to the feeling that fuels your desire, you can embrace the emotion that anchors your vision and brings it to fruition. That emotion grounds your desire and strengthens your intention. Then, as you show gratitude and release your intention to the universe, you set in motion the goal you seek to embrace.

Take inventory and control over your thoughts. For example, what makes you happy when you think about purchasing a new home? How does it make you feel when you envision how big your new home will be? Do you see how happy your family is with the space you imagine everyone will have in that home?

To make your visualization a reality, you need to connect the emotions behind what you want to the thoughts and the vision. The universe reacts to emotions, not just to your wants, needs, and desires. This is a scientific method that is proven with mindset work. Visualize and create your reality. The Law of Attraction teaches us to act in spite of anything that appears to stand in your way. Act, believe, and then allow it to happen. Receive.

Work to shift those negative belief systems, and feel that you deserve what you are consciously creating. We all have done this on some level in the process of getting a new job, a new love interest, a new car, and so on. But in order to truly transform our lives for the better, we need to master our mindset consciously, become aware of our thought patterns, and take inventory of what we want to create.

Coming back full circle to the beginning of this chapter, changes need to start by eliminating bad habits, patterns, and limiting beliefs. I will admit that it took me some time to resolve issues in my life. I still have my bad days, but this brings me back to understanding that we all have a choice about how we feel and react.

We also have free will, which can be a challenge, because, let's face it, it is easier to just give up. We need purpose and desire to drive us to an abundant life. If you are unhappy because you have settled for less, stop denying your full potential. Stop telling yourself that you are not worth it. Believe you have the power to create what you want. When setting your intentions, trust they can be achieved. Then you can find the motivation and passion to make these changes your new reality. It helps to know you have learned, grown, and evolved, and in turn you will help others.

My Painful Path to Transformation and Discovery

My health issues started shortly after I left the military. I was out for a little over a year and had a few different jobs. I was contracted through the state in early April of 2013 to start working for a bridge construction company as a skilled carpenter. While on the job, I started noticing pain in my neck that got worse over time. For the first time in my life, I experienced numbness in my arms, fingers, legs, and feet. I had migraines and a stiff neck with massive backaches. I knew something was not right. It was like I literally woke up one day and felt pain, discomfort, and spasms in all my limbs.

That fall, several months after I started working as a carpenter, I was in a car accident. It was minor but I had an impact, which added to the pain I was already experiencing in my neck. I went to the hospital to get checked and have X-rays, MRI, and CAT scans done. As I sat in the emergency room waiting for the doctor to come back, I assumed I had whiplash. When he returned, the doctor said he found some issues with my cervical spine. He proceeded to tell me I had severe degenerative disk disease.

I could not believe what I was hearing. I had no clue what that diagnosis meant for me. I was always an active person. My health was something I was proud of, and I got a lot of my confidence from being physically fit. I had my health to thank for the many achievements during my four years in the National Guard. I was deeply saddened to hear this news. It was devastating.

The ER doctor wanted me to follow up with my primary care physician, who ended up referring me to several specialists, neurologists, and neurosurgeons. I received treatment for my symptoms and physical therapy to help relieve them. I never dreamed within the span of two months I would have to go into surgery for a spinal fusion.

After weeks of appointments, I was scheduled for my spinal fusion on October 30, 2013. Weeks later, I learned the surgery had failed.

This was a big curve ball aimed straight at my head! I was sad, depressed, and had no clue where to start with getting my physical health back on track. I never thought this could happen to me! I was angry that it had, and there was nothing I could do about it. The sense of grief and loss came right back into my life again.

I had to take my time to process and accept the fact that I would never be the same again. I was going through the anger stage of grief. I felt guilty about being unable to do everything I used to for my family. I was mad because I really had no clue when I would be able to even get back to work. I wondered what kind of work I could do now. I had a lot to consider and knew that I had to figure out something.

One thing I was sure about: I wanted to help people and find a traditional way to do so. I started back to school to become a social worker in the fall of 2014. I always believed that we needed a formal education to be successful. That was a lie. Back then I was still stuck in the limiting beliefs I was taught and never thought for myself much. I still had much to learn.

Here I was starting all over again at 33 years old. I was clueless about what I really wanted, but at least I decided to give it a try. I was taking action to follow my short-term goals even if I did not know how. I wanted to be able to help people, and I thought the only legitimate way was through higher education. Going back to school as a nontraditional student was hard for me as I felt I did not fit in.

That was nothing new. I never fit in anywhere with anything I did. I tried to blend in but always felt something was missing. After I met a few locals who lived in my area and went to school with me, I got over feeling that I didn't belong. I was there to do my best and to learn. I spent the rest of my time with my family and looking for jobs that were related to the field I was studying.

Shortly after I started classes, I landed a job at one of the local behavioral and mental health psychiatrist offices. I worked closely with the patients, running a program as a decision support specialist before the patients saw the doctor. I got some experience working with all kinds of people with different diagnoses, and I became familiar with all the types of medications that were used to treat those conditions. I can't say I remember everything, but I learned from each patient and came to understand how case specific to each person treatment needed to be.

Although I did not realize it fully at the time, I felt like my identity had been taken from me after my diagnosis and failed surgery. I had to discover who I was at that point in my life. I was given an opportunity to choose again who I was and what I wanted to do. As I write this, I recall vividly how many times I felt uncomfortable and unhappy, but I recognize those experiences were great teachers, and all of them led me to become the person I am who thrives in the work that aligns with my purpose.

Becoming Your Higher Self

Through your life journeys, you have many opportunities to become your true higher self. That's true for all of us. Of course, at the time we're often clueless about that fact. The challenges we face are blessings in disguise! We all have our own way of gradually leveling up and evolving, but it is amazing how everything gets laid out to align us with our true purpose and path. We choose to go through experiences and troubled times to wake and shake up our spirit. The way I see it, we are forced to awaken through our discomfort. The natural state of being is movement. If we live in constant comfort, there is no reason to change or grow.

Even though I have had struggles and challenges, I know they have built my strength and helped me discover my truth. I have come through these obstacles, and now I want to be able to help others who face hardships. No matter what difficulties lie along our path, we have a choice to take aligned action for the life we deserve and want to create—a life of prosperity, financial freedom, and fulfillment.

After every challenge and loss, life goes on. If we do the best we can, we've made a great start. Each of us has a special place in this world, and this journey through life is our classroom. We are here to learn and grow as individuals and to collectively come together to help each other.

CHAPTER THREE

Manifesting What You Desire

Following the loss of my dad and dealing with both my own health issues and family medical situations, I made a decision to stop playing the victim role and take responsibility for my own thoughts and actions. Instead of waiting for life and these situations to get better, I decided to get help to align with my new goals and to kick off my business of helping others to heal. Once I released the role of victim, took responsibility for my own thoughts and actions, and realigned myself with what I wanted, my life changed.

If you too have come through many challenges and obstacles, you may be ready to recreate your own version of Heaven on Earth by manifesting what you truly desire. The truth is we are constantly manifesting. Our thoughts are powerful. We consciously and unconsciously create our reality. We have the power to create what we want or what we do not want.

I do not claim to know everything about this subject. What I can say is that I manifest easily. It comes naturally to me as I discovered after a few sessions with my business coach.

Recognizing Limiting Programming

The first step is to uncover conflicting beliefs, patterns, bad habits, and programming from your teachers and others in authority. We can become stuck in life and unable to move forward because of those old patterns. We get too comfortable with how we go about our day-to-day like the creatures of habit we are. I see people who live by society's standards too: graduate from high school, go to college, get a job, get married, and have some children. This can be a wonderful path if it is what you truly desire. Only you can discern if it is your path. You may have been told by parents this was the right thing to do, or societal norms may have influenced you to live what is considered appropriate. You have to ask yourself what it is *you* want.

We need to be brutally honest with ourselves. We all want to be happy. How do we evolve with all the complications that life throws at us and live in a natural state of being, a state that allows us to be okay with making necessary changes along our paths? We have total control over our choices and outcomes. I promise it is true!

Life has taught me that I am fully responsible for my own free will. So are you. We can all make choices in the direction that we have chosen to go. If you are like most of my clients, you probably have conformed to society's standards. Surely you know that there is so much more to life than living to work and pay bills and then die.

I always did what was necessary to survive. I came to realize that I had settled for less at times because I did not recognize my own self-worth. When I acknowledged that truth and recognized that I had a choice, I decided to make the necessary changes to manifest what I truly wanted. I was living a life with no purpose, the one that others expected of me. I was not happy. I had to look for different options and opportunities in order to find another path, to choose again.

Most of us were taught from childhood that if we worked hard to make a living we would be rewarded. What lies we were told by our teachers, parents, and bosses—that we needed to follow the same path they did. Wow! No wonder it took me so long to figure out what went wrong. Like all of us, I was programmed to believe this model was the only way.

When I looked back on all I was taught, I understood where my limiting beliefs stemmed from. Even having a certain religious background can instill those patterns. There are so many ways in which society has constrained our thinking. I have worked with many clients whose limiting systems dramatically affected their lives. Recognizing this is not to place blame on anyone. Those who raised and trained us to restrict our life choices never intended harm. They did their best to help us. It is so important to forgive. Forgive yourself first and forgive those who hurt you, not for them but because doing so will free you from the chains of past wounds.

Mastermind Manifesting

We don't have to continue adhering to the teachings that have restrained our joy. Exploring how to start manifesting is exciting and fun. This process uses a mixture of energy work, mindset reprogramming, and knowing your value. It is well worth the effort, and you can use a number of tools and modalities. My course, Mastermind Manifesting, shares the methods for success. You can use these tools in your everyday life in every area for the rest of your years.

Here is the process that I take my clients through to start teaching them what they need to successfully and consciously create. It all starts with defining a short-term goal and a plan. As I mentioned in the previous chapter, it's best to start small at first and take baby steps.

Ask yourself, "What do I truly want?" Be honest with yourself when you answer. Then ask, "*Why* do I want it?" What is it that connects you *emotionally* to this desire?

Connecting the *why* with the *what* is the most important piece of the puzzle. Many people have a hard time manifesting because they miss this vital step. Why is this part essential? The emotion creates the fuel for the fire. Your thoughts are your fire, but only your feelings can truly ignite them.

You can choose to create what you want by putting your emotion, particularly joy and happiness, behind your thought or vision. Joy and happiness are the highest frequencies on the emotional scale when manifesting. Get excited about the prospect of your vision becoming reality! If you want your goal badly enough and it excites you, then you have created the ideal fuel for the fire.

Discovering and understanding your daily patterns, bad habits, and conflicting beliefs leads you to the recognition that something has to change. You need to get out of your comfort zone. Change allows a new result to take shape. What can you do differently to receive a better outcome? Set some clear intentions geared toward achieving your goal and receiving your desire.

Universal law says that where there is a desire, a way has already been made. Everything you want already exists and is waiting for you. That is the law. You may not see it because negative emotional junk gets in the way. But universal law states that whatever you ask to receive is freely given.

Somewhere along the way, most of us stopped listening to our own soul. We began seeking in others and reaching for things on the outside to help us navigate life's journey. We actually need to go within first to find solutions and heal ourselves. Only we can shut ourselves off from the universal flow of energy, which streams to us all the time. Whether you believe it or not, that flow is ceaseless, and the universe is always listening to every thought. Be careful what you imagine and say because the universe can sense each word and mental picture.

It took me more than 15 years to work through my healing journey, get clear about my desires, and align with my purpose. I had to dig deeply within and get into some deep, dark work. I noticed that most of the emotional baggage I had carried around with me started from an early age. I am a survivor of both child sexual abuse and rape.

I blamed myself for everything that happened to me. Growing up, I was constantly in counseling and worked with therapists off and on until 2019. You get closer to what you want as you work on yourself and learn your self-worth. My journey back to my truth was a gradual, meaningful process.

Your path to clear and heal your "junk" may be totally different from mine. If you are willing to change and find the support you need, you'll be amazed at what you can manifest in your life.

Clearing and healing the past trauma that is getting in your way is the second step, which is called *shifting*. I use several tools with my clients to help them identify and bring out consciously what may not be seen or understood on the surface. I have had clients with major breakthroughs after this kind of healing and energy work.

This shifting process helps uncover the root cause of life situations that play out as repeated patterns. Powerful transformations come from consciously shifting related issues you probably have not been aware of previously. Everything is interconnected. Carrying the burdens of your past always affects your present. You cannot hold onto what no longer serves you and still get where you want to be in the future.

Here are some of those key pieces to the process of creating the life you want:

- Manifesting is easy when you state your intentions clearly and connect the *what* (your goal or desired outcome) with the *why* (the feeling that leads you to want that outcome). Define what you want and why.
- Connect your emotions and the feeling of joy and happiness with your vision for the future. Sustain the joy as you hold the vision.
- Thoughts are powerful. Keep the positive ones in the forefront and negative thoughts in check.
- Do not waste time and energy on the negative. Acknowledge those undesirable thoughts and let them go.
- Take new and different actions to get better results.

We work on reading the evidence on the realistic, tangible level of the physical, third-dimensional world. Using the universal energy and allowing it to work for you and with you is key. Now we are learning, growing, and having breakthroughs.

Be okay with being perfectly imperfect. This step requires you to take aligned, inspired action. If the initial results are not quite what you intended, you will act and assess, maybe even adjust. It is completely okay to do so. After you take new actions, the evidence shows up. You will have as many attempts as necessary to course correct if the outcomes do not meet your expectations.

Focus on the details of what you want. As you make adjustments to your course of action or incorporate additional strategies, you can achieve better outcomes. Be happy and let it happen! Yes, this is the point at which most give up. If you have thought about what you desire and you're connected to the *feeling* of why you want it, then it should manifest quickly, right? Wrong. Depending on what you asked for and how many pieces of that puzzle need to fit together to create the outcome of you want, it may take some time.

I am impatient. I know it can be hard to wait for the results you seek. Let it happen. Do not stop trusting your decisions and taking action, continually asking when or how in the world it will happen. Get my drift? Second guessing yourself and the universe will not help to speed things along. Instead, such behavior will create a block to allowing the natural process of receiving what you asked for. Yes, that is right! See it, feel it, and *let it happen*.

My coach taught me to leave it to the universe. I took that advice. As a result, I have not had any issues other than changing my mind and adding a few more details to my plan. Keep in mind that you can go back and readjust what you originally intended. We have many opportunities to create and alter our plans if we choose. Once you have set the process in motion, you can relax and allow the universe to take care of you and simply be open to receive.

I suggest you engage a coach who you aspire to be. Make sure there is an energetic match—that your energies mesh well together. Work with those who inspire you and with whom you have many interests, values, and beliefs in common. By following this advice, I have manifested some big opportunities since starting my business professionally.

Here is one client's story of how she used this process to manifest what she truly wanted.

> *I found myself unconsciously bringing things I did not want into my life. I was stopping just before it was time to take the leap at success. I told myself that if I get too big, it would not be fun. That would mean my passion turned into "work" and "work" requires a great deal of commitment and responsibility. Another story I told myself was, "I am not good enough."*

Obviously, something needed to change, or I would be stuck in this place. I had goals in mind that I wanted to make real.

Connecting my emotions and the feeling of joy and happiness that would come when these goals were real made a huge difference! It enabled me to take aligned action to create my results.

Next I retrained my mind and started taking better care of my body. I had let both of these things fall by the wayside as I was trying to balance my pain from an accident with taking care of myself. Clearly I was out of balance mentally, spiritually, and physically.

I worked on identifying the blocks and patterns that didn't serve my higher self. These were the things that kept me from manifesting what I genuinely wanted consistently. Working on both my mind and body gave me confidence in my skills and abilities and allowed me to start trusting my spiritual gifts, knowing I could help others. I let go of my fear of attracting prosperity and replaced it with knowing I am worthy of what I desire in my life.

I gave one hundred percent and showed up for myself. I invested in myself and my learning and took responsibility for how to navigate my way through this new process.

Honestly, I was astounded at how fast my results came in! While working through the different processes

I needed, all areas of life flowed and came into alignment.

I learned not be concerned about how the money will come and to trust the process. I literally had written down a financial number of what I wanted and put it out there to the universe with my intent. I woke up the next morning with that exact dollar amount! That's all the proof I needed to continue using the manifesting process. I now use this in my everyday life and learn something new as I grow.

Lisa has continued with me for private coaching. She has been working on her business plans and adding to her extensive resumé. It has been amazing to watch her develop her psychic mediumship skills and blend these with her healing work. Her passion for helping others has helped her align to her higher self. Once we take the time to know ourselves, our wants, needs, and desires *first*, then we can serve others on a greater level.

> *"Our psyche can function as though space did not exist. The psyche can thus be independent of space, of time, and of causality. This explains the possibility of magic."*
>
> —Carl Jung

CHAPTER FOUR

Energy Work

Everything is energy. Energy is the vital life force of everything in the universe. Whether we realize it or not, we all work with energy every day.

Here is an easy explanation. Energy carries a vibration. Money, my voice, music—all are forms of energy that emit a frequency. There is positive and negative energy, and there are higher and lower vibrations. We all radiate an energy field around our physical body. We call this the aura. Within this energy field, we hold impressions of our experiences from this life and past lifetimes.

The aura is made up of our physical, emotional, mental, and spiritual bodies. The energy field around our body contains all these levels of experience. Spirits then can relate their experiences through us.

Developing energetic balance helps us stay grounded and protected. We are constantly giving and taking energy every second of the day—even when we are not consciously aware of it.

How Our Energy System Works

The first step to realization is becoming aware of how you feel. Are you tired when you hang out with a friend who is always unhappy or has a problem for every solution? Notice how you feel when you interact with people in your family or friends and even strangers. This will help you understand how your energy is being directed and how it meshes with the energy of those around you.

If you find yourself exhausted after spending time with other people, my best advice is to learn to ground and protect your energy field. When you feel drained from interacting with these individuals, it's time to put your boundaries up. You are having a negative energy exchange. Other examples of this phenomenon could be feeling angry for no reason while you're at work or feeling out of balance when you give time to those who don't give energy back to you. You should prepare for these occasions by protecting yourself and recharging for the day.

Some ways of protecting your own energy for the day include:

1. Visualizing a bubble of white light around you before you interact with anyone

2. Praying to God or the Creator
3. Asking the angels to assist you to keep your energy protected
4. Talking to your gatekeeper, a main guide who keeps negative energy away from you.

As you can see, we have options. You just have to choose what works best for you.

Centering Yourself with the Breath

Breath work is essential to connecting with your own rhythm of respiration. This technique can bring you to center quickly and you can do it anywhere. I often use my breathing when I engage with negative people or a negative space. I re-center, recharge, and re-ground. Imagine beautiful white light filling your lungs and clearing anything that does not serve your higher self. Let it fill your entire body until you radiate with light. Take a few seconds to breathe slowly and deeply as you envision that purifying energy flowing through you until you feel clear, strong, and balanced.

The first steps of my work with clients are to teach them techniques to identify how their soul feels. We need to rewire and reconnect with who we are by remembering what our own energy feels like. These techniques begin to retrain your focus and improve your energy. Grounding work is vital to this process.

Life can be demanding, which makes it essential to set some *me time* aside to still your mind. Many of my clients give me feedback about not having time to themselves. We all have so many excuses to not do what is best for us. I was one of those busy people too, so I understand how this happens. Just start with a few minutes a day to sit in silence. You can listen to uplifting music and close your eyes. Mastering and identifying self is key to enhancing positive energy plus beneficial results in your life.

Meditation allows you to tune into your energy. So many people have told me, "I cannot sit and meditate." I have to laugh when I hear that because most are already shifting into a slower brainwave state in ways they don't consider "meditation." I meditated without knowing it for the longest time. I lay in the pool and relaxed, listening to my music. Refreshing, right? Yes, we even do it while we drive when melodic music is playing. Without recognizing it, everyone meditates at some point in some way. It is so natural for us that we have no clue we do it. Imagine that.

If you begin to consciously meditate on a regular basis, imagine how far you can go—especially for those who want to further your spiritual growth and development. I like to make the process fun and interesting. I am an expressive, creative person and love a good challenge. I challenged myself to find the method that worked best for me, and now I look forward to my daily meditations. When you discover the form of meditation that brings you the greatest comfort, you will love the sense of connection that comes from this gift to yourself.

How I choose to meditate looks something like this. I sit in nature, plant my bare feet in the grass to ground, and connect to Mother Earth. Then I put on a play list and set my intentions for my purpose of connecting. I could be sitting with my guides ready to work with me or simply charging my energy for the day. I listen to Native American drumming to raise my vibration. I love how the beat makes me feel. I want you to feel the joy that I do when you connect, so I'm sharing this meditation to help you join with your own energy.

Meditation: The Essence of Your Spirit Being

This meditation invites you to recognize and remember the beautiful, perfect soul that you are. You are a part of the Source of Creation and the universal life force. It's time to connect with your own unique essence.

Find a comfortable space to sit and ground into Mother Earth. Sit anywhere that you can have the base of your spine or feet touching the ground in order to connect the root chakra to the Earth. If you can sit barefoot in the grass or in nature, that would be ideal but is not essential. Anywhere will work.

Clear your mind and close your eyes. Take a deep breath in through your nose to the count of seven. Exhale out of your mouth ever so slowly until you can no longer push air out. Remember you are safe and protected by the white light. You are loved and so beautiful.

As you inhale through your nose, imagine you are breathing in a brilliant white light that is filling the center of your chest as you breathe. Allow this light to move through you, slowly expanding through your entire being. Take another deep breath in to the count of seven. Feel your lungs and your stomach expand and draw in the healing properties of the white light. Breathe out and let your belly relax naturally.

Feel yourself beginning to center, to release all cares. Give yourself permission to receive this beautiful gift always offered freely and constantly available to you. One more time: deep breath in through your nose to the count of seven and gradually release out of your mouth so the exhale is almost twice as long as the inhale. Let this be a time to relax and receive—nothing more.

Now continue your normal breathing rhythm. Focus your awareness on the center of the chest where your light is so bright. Now this light and power wants to shine out past your frame. Start to notice the feeling of that expansive energy, of your own loving, caring soul that is strong and brilliant. Your inner light grows more powerful as you bring your attention to it. This is your essence—who you truly are—your spiritual self. Sense that energy magnifying out to fill the room. You have created your safe space where you truly can be yourself. You are divine and you are beautiful.

Bring your awareness to the space where you're sitting. Notice how you feel in your physical body. Feel the chair or the ground where you sit. Focus your energy on the ground. Envision roots growing out of your feet or the base of your spine as if you were a tree reaching down. Push those roots down into Mother Earth.

As your roots extend downward into Mother Earth, your energy shifts. Allow your stress, anxiety, and any pain to flow out through your roots. Let the Earth absorb anything that no longer servers your higher self. Mother Earth can recycle all the negative energy into the soil.

Now imagine your roots wrapping around a beautiful crystal. The Earth's energy can now flow up into your energy centers. Feel the current of energy as it rises from the planet up through your feet and your calves to your hips. Sense yourself relaxing more as the light travels up to the stomach and your feeling of tension from the day, the week, your life releases. You are happy and so relaxed.

As the loving light of Mother Earth continues to flow up through your body, welcome its gentle energy into your heart. Let it expand through your chest and upper torso.

As it moves up to the throat area, allow this calming energy to pour through your shoulders, your forearms, and down to your fingertips.

This nurturing essence continues to rise in your body into your head and face. Notice if your jaw is tense. If so, relax that area and drop your jaw. Unclench your teeth and let your face muscles slacken. Let the tension melt away from your eyes and soften your gaze. Focus between your eyebrows and allow yourself to see the shimmering light work on this area for a few moments. Finally, move to the space above your head.

There the light of Source, the divine essence of the universe, merges with your light. Visualize this brilliant white light building as you're radiating its power. Feel this vibrant power rushing through and around you. At this point, you may sense the energy shift as your vibration rises. Envision an image of your soul shining the brightest light you have ever seen. Within that brilliant essence, you feel safe and loved.

The universe is merging with your unique light. You see a shining gold light blending with your energy. This is the part of you that has always been. You are connected and tapped into the divine—a spiritual being united with all things. Feel this pure love of the Creator that knows you better than you know yourself and is suppling you with all the energy, love, and support you need. Let that love embrace you and give you what you seek most.

Just sit in this energy and observe how you feel. Sense your energy. Take some deep breaths. Let yourself bask in this feeling. You are still safe and relaxed. Allow your energy to build as you sit, still visualizing your brilliant light and blending with the universal Source. See yourself glowing as the radiance of your being spins together with that of Source and the Earth.

Sit in this light for as long as you want until your energy feels balanced, protected, and fully recharged. Then take another deep breath in through your nose and back out through your mouth. Come back to your everyday awareness. Thank the Creator and all light beings from the other side for their help.

This process grounds, balances, and recharges your seven main physical energy hubs. Remember you may come back to this meditation any time you want.

Your Spiritual Toolkit: 20 Steps to Raise Your Vibration

Everything has a vibration, including us. We are energetic beings with an aura comprised of physical, etheric, emotional, mental, and spiritual levels—each of which has its own vibration. When in alignment, these create the positive vibration of our being. Sometimes these levels are out of alignment and vibrate at lower or higher frequencies. When our life spins out of control in certain areas, we need to address the shifts in our energy and realign our energy levels.

I tune in to a client's vibration and energy field to find the root cause of blocks, obstacles, and so on. You can adjust your energy systems when they become overactive or underactive. Look at what is showing up in your life currently in order to identify what is out of balance. When you bring conscious awareness to a situation and identify where you are struggling, you can change the flow of the energy.

Tools for spiritual protection, cleansing, and purifying include tending to our basic needs such as self-care, water, healthy diet, sleep, and awareness of environmental factors. We receive or exchange energy from everything and everyone. Consider all possibilities for energy depletion and recognize where and when this happens. Knowledge is wisdom. We get so busy with life we forget to acknowledge this as a major factor to put into the equation of our health and wellbeing.

The goal is to stay in a higher vibration, and all the spiritual tools are essential to do this. We use our toolbox to help keep us in a positive state. This kit helps us to check what is energetically draining us. Here are some tips and tools for maintaining a positive mindset and a healthy vibration:

1. Be grateful for what you already have. This is the most important step. Say to yourself, "I am

abundant and have all that I want now." Write down 10 things that you are grateful for. Journaling can be a great way to help shift your perspective. I do a process of gratitude for 21 days when I want to really raise my vibration.

2. Do one or more random acts of kindness daily. Smile and give someone a compliment. Donate, support others, and be kind.
3. Listen to uplifting music.
4. Meditate.
5. Laugh as much as you can. Joy carries the highest vibration.
6. Dance. Move your physical body. Don't let your energy get stagnant.
7. Be present and appreciate the beauty around you.
8. Drink water.
9. Eat clean, organic foods.
10. Practice self-love and self-care. Take an Epsom salt bath.
11. Maintain healthy boundaries. Say "no" to that which drains your energy.
12. Disconnect from electronics and reconnect with nature.
13. Do one thing differently from the day before.

14. Declutter your workspace and your home.
15. Go out with friends who make you laugh and feel happy.
16. Show love to your family. Hug your loved ones.
17. Watch a funny movie.
18. Do some breath work.
19. Give yourself permission to treat yourself to whatever you desire one day a week.
20. Get out of your head and be happy, my friends.

Using these tools regularly will bring a heightened awareness of our own energy and help us recognize when we are depleted.

We also need to pay attention to our energy in the moment and remain accountable for all our interactions throughout the day. If we do not know why we feel drained, how can we prevent energetic attacks? It's easy to go through life on autopilot, but staying attuned to your energy and that of those around you will provide a better understanding of the vibrations that affect you and give you insight into shifting what doesn't work for your benefit.

Boundaries are a great start to establish protection of your energy field. We begin to build boundaries with people who are part of our everyday life—co-workers, family members, friends. We all have good, bad, and life-sucking relationships. We've all encountered energetic vampires who take our energy and/or leave us with a sticky blob of residue in our energy field that looks like sludge and is dull and ugly.

It is perfectly okay to tell someone "no" when they are constantly asking for your time and energy for their own benefit only. Those who consistently take rather than exchange energy are creating an imbalance, which is wrong on many levels. Give yourself permission to remove yourself from those kinds of people.

Healthy relationships require an equal exchange of energy. When the flow of energy becomes out of balance, this does not serve you. When you feel defeated and depleted, run! A constant exchange of positive energy creates a mutually beneficial relationship. Vampiric relationships, on the other hand, leave you feeling completely drained after every encounter. Why waste your precious time and energy on those who perpetuate imbalance?

Setting Healthy Boundaries

One of my clients shared concern about her relationship with her daughter, who lived in a different state. She told me she had to beg to see her granddaughter and rarely heard from her daughter. This pained her deeply because she did not understand why the relationship felt so distant. She blamed herself for her daughter and granddaughter not calling or coming to visit. It was important to her to have a close bond with them both.

This is an example of how to set healthy boundaries. During the session, she explained how her daughter only contacted her when she needed money. I asked her how that made her feel. She said she felt used and not good enough unless she could help her. I see this all the time and it is sad to know that this happens.

How do we handle a situation like this when one person is not getting the love she wants and deserves in return? We need to learn that we have no way to control others. The answer relates to self-worth.

First, be willing to let go of what you cannot control. Please do not allow yourself to be emotionally drained and used because of the role others expect you to play. Do not allow someone to hurt you continuously. We need to value our worth and be clear about what we deserve. Make the choice to stand your ground and set those healthy boundaries.

My client began to realize that she had bad habits and discovered patterns she did not see before our sessions. When we get support, it helps us view our lives from a clearer perspective. My client knew something had to change to break those patterns and habits.

Many times, the answers we all seek are so simple, but we choose to see what we want. Learning to set boundaries is a healthy way to protect yourself. You will see positive proof after you make the choice to take a different action.

My client was giving her daughter money whenever she called. She chose to stop. It was a small step, but she felt better for having made it. At the same time, her daughter came to realize that what her mom really wanted was to spend more time with her and her child. Her daughter started making time for her mother, which shifted their relationship in a major way. They are now working on how to communicate more openly and plan more visits.

We can start to heal and learn how to protect ourselves from unhealthy situations. Do not allow someone to take advantage of you. Be aware of how you feel after interacting with those you love. Sometimes we set ourselves up by not knowing any better. Guilt plays a big role. Do not feel guilty if you need to make changes to any relationship to do what is best for you.

> *"If you want to know the secrets to the universe, think in terms of energy, frequency and vibration."*
>
> —Nikola Tesla

Personal Reflections

What visions of hope or inspired messages did you receive from your meditations?

How do you protect your energy?
Write out what works for you here.

Create your opening ritual in your own powerful words. Your intent is most important and the energy in your voice and words is your magic.

CHAPTER FIVE

Working with Your Spirit Guides

Did you know that we have a team of spirit guides who are joined to us at birth?

As we become more aware of our individual journey and our purpose, we can incorporate more understanding about how our guides work specifically with us. We draw those guides to us who align with our mission. As we progress toward our goals and raise our vibrations, we align with spirit beings who will direct us toward moving forward at each stage. They do not intrude; we must ask them specifically for their help.

Our spirit helpers include the following members of our team.

- Deceased Loved Ones: The most common type of spirit guide is a loved one in spirit. Grandparents often fill that role. We may or may not have known them in this lifetime, but we made an agreement that they would watch over and help us once they passed to the other side. Other familial spirit guides include children who had a short life but were highly evolved spiritual beings who taught us something with their gift and blessing to choose us as their parents.

- Past Life Friends and Family: These are also referred to as our soul group. Some choose to volunteer for periods of time to help teach us lessons about relationships. These relate to the little details etched into our blueprints before we incarnate. Like the saying goes, you either learned from the experience or had to work out some issues that were not resolved in a past life.

- Ancestors: The bloodline is important in many ways including morals, values, and beliefs we carry over from generations past. Our ancestors choose to watch over us, protect us, and teach traditions related to our family history.

- General Spirit Helpers: These are experts on the other side that volunteered to take on your case in a specific area to help you learn or work through challenges. Most likely we never lived a past life with them.

- Ascended Masters: Ascended Masters are more evolved and have completed all higher levels of training and finished their master's degree so to speak. Buddha, Mother Mary, Jesus, and saints fall into this category. They have lived on Earth and risen beyond the issues we face here.

- Spirit Animals: Spirit animal guides could include a pet you had in this lifetime and those that have reincarnated with you over several lifetimes and in many different forms. Some may reveal themselves to you as signs or symbols. Even their color has meaning. Animals represent specific wisdom, and every species has a particular significance. They assist, support, and guide you through different stages and levels of life. As you grow and evolve, some of your animal guides may change.
- Angels: There are guardian angels, archangels, and many other levels of angelic beings all the way up to the cherubim and seraphim. Angels are pure beings of light.
- Elementals and Nature Spirits: This category includes mermaids, elves, fairies, and other "mystical and mythical" beings, which some call Earth angels.

Working with Your Guides

We all come here to experience, evolve, learn soul lessons, clear past traumas and debts from other lifetimes, and complete our life task or purpose.

When we went to school, we had different teachers for different subjects. All of our schoolteachers and professors had specialties they taught. Similarly, we have a team or a group of guides and angels who fulfill different roles to help us through a variety of life experiences.

We each have a main guide who heads our team. Some spirit guides assist us without our awareness during everyday life. Some come to help with a particular task at hand. When you begin a new venture, for example, a spirit helper may come into your life to support you through issues you may encounter.

The difference between an angel and a spirit guide is that angels have never been human. They've never incarnated. We can have many types of guides. All have their own role, and many factors go into determining the different types of guides and the functions or jobs those guides perform on your team.

Your Blueprint

Each of us enters into this life with a unique energetic blueprint. Included in your energetic makeup is your archetype, the elements you are drawn to (air, water, fire, earth, ether), your strongest chakra, the colors of your aura, and all the things that make you, you—your soul personality and the feel of your energy.

The spirit world sees and identifies us by our energy, not by the shell of the human body. Your guides are an energetic match for you. While they may be significantly more evolved in some cases, their energy will mesh with yours. The ones you do not know from this life (who aren't grandparents or other loved ones in spirit) or whom you haven't encountered in a past life will be guides whose energy relates to yours. They see and identify with your blueprint. They may have shared a similar path and purpose in past lives and hold great insight into your own. These spirit guides become a part of your team because of that energetic match.

Pre-incarnation Agreements

When we incarnate, we don't always come with our whole soul group. Some choose to stay behind to help us from spirit. They have made pre-incarnation agreements with us to help while we are here on Earth.

These souls are often past life friends who have consented to assist us during our time in the physical world. We make these soul agreements before we are born. Some soul contracts even last many lifetimes if we do not achieve what we intended in a particular life. We set an intention to evolve in each life. While we're still in spirit, we think this will be an easy purpose to accomplish. Of course, it doesn't always turn out to be as simple as we imagined when we were still beings of light.

Ties with those in spirit include blood or emotional relationships. Ancestors who have been in the spirit realm for some time still connect to us here, and deceased loved ones whom we have known in this lifetime may have chosen to leave their own lives early in order to act as guides for us and help us to evolve to a higher level.

Sometimes even those with whom we have had horrible encounters may move to a different level after they depart the physical. From the other side, they can try to support us by working as our guides.

Attaining knowledge and gaining a higher frequency are important because the guides we have match our level of understanding and our resonance. The guides who are supposed to teach us or advance our spiritual growth are appropriate to our degree of understanding and vibration. That means we are not going to get the college professor of guides if we're still at the high school stage of learning. As we evolve, our guides change and adjust according to our needs.

In addition to the spirit helpers listed earlier, these are important members of our spiritual team.

- Master Guide: This is the manager of your spirit team. You will work with this guide frequently, and his or her role is to delegate to the others. This spirit is your go-to guide whenever you need insight or support.
- Gatekeeper: This guide is your doorman, your bouncer. He or she is here to protect you and keep

you safe. Gatekeepers ensure you are guarded while working with energies, specifically negative entities, and protect you against intrusion by groups of spirits and their energy.

- Teacher: My favorites are the mentor guides who assist with your soul's growth and teach you things related to the life lessons you're here to learn.
- Relationship: These guides act as counselors on your team. They help navigate your interpersonal relationships to bring people together to clear and heal past life debts and to find peace.
- Helper: These guides aid you with specific tasks, projects, and new ideas. They are the consultants on your team and often come to assist you for a period of time when you begin a new path or project.
- Healer: These are responsible for healing your energy field and balancing your chakras. They are the medics that help teach you how to heal yourself and others.

Your task is to connect to your team of spirit guides. Meditating will help you make that connection. Set your intentions prior to meditation. Understand that linking to your spirit helpers through meditation is not always successful the first time you try. It could take some practice to identify your guides and sense their distinctive energy and purpose. My wish is to help you slowly learn to work more directly with your team so they can guide you forward at each stage.

Meditation: Connecting with Your Guides

The first part of this repeats the process used in the previous meditation. Begin by getting yourself into a comfortable position. Close your eyes, take a deep breath through your nose, and exhale gradually through your mouth. (Your out-breath should be so slow it takes almost twice as long as the inhale.) Drop your shoulders and relax even more with every exhale. When you are taking a deep breath, imagine inhaling that brilliant white healing light into your lungs and visualize it moving throughout your whole body.

As you are breathing out of your mouth, you are becoming even more relaxed. Feel your jaw unclench and drop. Imagine every breath cleansing you. The white light has healing qualities that will help you let go of all tension and welcome restorative energy.

Repeat this breathing process three times. Then bring your respiration back to its normal rhythm. Start to see roots going down into Mother Earth from the bottom of your feet. Direct your roots deep into the ground as far as you can send them.

Notice how you feel as you sink those roots into the soil. Can you sense this grounding you? You should feel that natural pull from Mother Earth. She is taking what no longer serves your higher self and recycling the sludge from your energy field. Envision her sending gold, sparkling energy back up through those roots to replenish you, supplying balancing and grounding protection for you.

Bring your awareness to the center of your chest and visualize the white light there spreading to fill your entire being. Feel this light expanding outside your physical body and wanting to shine as far as it can. With your inner sight, look at your spiritual being radiating within this beautiful white light.

Feel the energy build and magnify the light to call to the universe. Notice an even brighter light with a golden hue come to meet your light. This is the light of the Creator embracing you with a feeling of peace, love, and support. You are now connected to the other side. You are safe and loved.

Let yourself feel completely serene and at peace. Then imagine yourself at the ocean. See the waves as you look towards the horizon. Smell the salt in the air as the tides wash ashore to where you are standing. Look down and see the water as it touches your feet. Feel its warmth as it splashes over your feet on the hot sand.

Walk down the beach, watching your feet sink into the warm, wet sand. Feel the sand between your toes. Soft sand gives way under your feet and water rushes over toes as you continue to walk.

Turn to look out at the ocean and notice how blue the water is. The sun overhead causes the sea to sparkle and shimmer with light, glistening like magic as it reflects the sun's rays. Seeing this fills your heart with happiness and joy. This is your sanctuary, where you are safe and relaxed, your haven that feels like home—sheltered, loved, and always protected.

Continue to stroll along your beach for a while, feeling at peace, contented, and happy. Notice the soft, warm sand beneath your feet, the water rushing over your toes.

Up ahead you spot a path that goes into a large, wooded area and follow that trail through an opening that calls you into the forest. As you move along the path, look around you at the trees, smell the scents of pine, eucalyptus, and grass. The sound of the waves becomes distant now. Your attention is drawn to the beautiful, vibrant flowers that line your path. Birds light on nearby tree branches. The sun shines down on you through the trees, and a warm breeze touches your skin. Feel it. Listen to the birds singing above you in the trees. Butterflies dance all around you as you lean over to smell the flowers just off the path. Ahead of you in the distance, you see a clearing. Walk into this glade, where lush yellow flowers grow. They are everywhere as far as you can see.

When you stop to smell them, the scent brings back a memory. You recall a loved one who is in spirit. You remember that special person who now lives in the spirit world, someone you knew and loved.

You look up and see the birds and butterflies again. Can you hear the birds? Can you get close enough to the butterflies to touch them? Enjoy being here walking through this beautiful field of yellow flowers and nature. You feel calm, at peace, and relaxed.

As you continue your walk, you notice the shape of a person walking towards you from the distance. They are getting closer and closer. Finally, you recognize them. You see it is your special person, the one who now lives in spirit. They come to stand right in front of you. Your heart is beating with joy and love for this person. You gaze at their smile, their beautiful face, and warm eyes. They are raising their arms to greet you and hold you tight. You embrace your special person, feeling how strong the bond of love is. Powerful, strong loving joy.

Let the happiness and joy wash over you as you hold this person you love and miss so much. Spend this time with your loved one. Walk through the field together. Take as much time as you need to chat and catch up. Ask them what you want to know and *listen*. They will answer you and tell you they are always near you, guiding and helping you. Take their arm and walk together for as long as you need to.

After you have shared whatever you need to with each other, the time comes for your loved one to go back *home*. Until you can meet again, you embrace each other and etch the memory of their smile on your consciousness. Be grateful once more for your connection. You now know at any time you may always come back to this special meeting place you have created. You can return to this safe space to see them whenever you want or need.

Watch them turn away now and leave the way they came. Then head back through the fields of the lush yellow flowers and return along the pathway that brought you here, watching the butterflies dance around you and hearing the birds singing as you move back out of the forest. The scent of the flowers fills your senses. Your heart is filled with joy, peace, and love.

Looking up at the pine trees, smell the earthy scent of nature in the air. Notice the dirt path beneath you. Look down and see the tree roots as you navigate around them. You are getting close to the beach again. Can you hear the waves getting louder? You look up again and see the white sand and the sun shining on the water.

Back on your private strand of beach, you drink in the color of the sea. Smell the salt in the air and feel the sand and the warm water under your feet again. Take one last look around. You are happy and at peace as you never have been before. You now know your loved ones are at peace too—happy, and never far away. You can always visit with them, and, if you listen, you can always hear them. Take a deep breath in through your nose and very slowly exhale it through your mouth.

Transport yourself back into the room. Bring joy, love, and peace with you. Take a few breaths and feel the chair where you sit. Notice your awareness returning to its normal state with all the daily thoughts slowly returning to your mind. Wiggle your fingers and toes and open your eyes when you are ready. Be at peace and give thanks for this beautiful visit and connection you have learned to make.

As mentioned earlier, you will want to set your intentions prior to the meditation. You may use this same visualization or guided journey to meet with your main spirit guide, your relationship guide, your ancestors, healing helpers, or any of your other team members. The more you practice meditating, the easier it will become to access your spirit helpers and deepen that connection with them. This is a wonderful method for reaching out to loved ones on the other side or communicating with any of your other guides, angels, and helpers.

PART II

My Journey Through the Dark

CHAPTER SIX

My Intuitive Journey

I have been on a spiritual journey since I was young. From an early age, I saw, felt, sensed, and experienced things others did not. As soon as I was old enough, I started to educate myself by reading books on metaphysical subjects. I wanted to understand what I was never taught. I did not have anyone to guide me or help me appreciate and use my gifts.

I was baptized a Methodist. My father was Catholic. My parents allowed me to explore on my own. I was never forced to choose what I believed and never saw different religions as contradicting each other. I understood their messages shared the same purpose. It did not matter what place you chose to worship or what denomination you were.

In my early years I often found myself at church, Bible school, or CYC, an after-school program run by the church where I attended Sunday services regularly. I liked getting out on a weekday and was curious about what they taught. After services, we could go into a room for arts and crafts, which I loved. It was an outlet for me to be creative—one reason I continued to attend for years.

As I tried to understand religion from other people's viewpoints. I desperately searched for answers to understand what I felt in my soul but couldn't explain in words. I kept hoping I would hear something tied to my own personal experience, but that never happened. While I respected their beliefs and perspectives, they did not resonate with me. I always left with more questions—confused and feeling alone.

Around the age of 12, after years of going but never finding what I was searching for, I stopped attending church regularly. I chose to share my experiences with very few people—only with my fellow black sheep and misfits.

The Spirits in the Yellow House

Growing up, I lived in a ranch-style house with one floor and a full basement on a double corner lot. This was my dad's parents' home. My father's side of the family was Italian. There were five of us living there together: my older brother, my pap, Mom, Dad, and me.

My dad's mom, Elizabeth Aaron Malino, had gotten sick while they lived in the house. She passed away at home with stage four colon cancer when my dad was still young. She was in her early 40s. My grandfather never remarried.

Elizabeth was my paternal grandmother. As a spirit she has been with me since I was born. I never knew her in this lifetime. Whenever I felt loving, peaceful energy around me, I knew she was there; I saw and sensed her. She watched me grow up and kept a close eye on our family. I did a painting of her when I was about 17. I painted her as I saw her and based on what I could feel from her.

Growing up in that house was not always fun. I saw and heard spirits from a young age. I could feel their sadness or fear but could not make out what they were saying. This traumatized me as a child, filling me with fear. I was afraid of the dark and of mirrors and hated bedtime. Many nights I was awakened by someone or something. My blankets would get ripped off. I would see people all around my bed just staring at me. I did not realize that others could not see them. No one believed me when I tried to talk about what I saw and experienced.

My supernatural experiences were not limited to the house though. I had them everywhere I went. During the daytime I perceived spirits around other people. These souls looked the same as everyone else. They were not transparent or ghostly in appearance. At the time I didn't realize they were my dead relatives that had been gone for years.

The older I got the more persistent the spirits were. Although I did not always see them as clearly as when I was younger, I started to have more intense feelings. I often sensed fear from them and a deep sadness. I could not understand why my perceptions of them were changing. How can a young person process this kind of experience? Even with these encounters, I always felt loving energy surrounding me as a young child until a big energy shift happened around my whole family.

Growing up, I felt deeply loved by both of my grandfathers. They were my favorite people. My pap (my paternal grandfather) babysat me when everyone else was at work. My mom's father, Donald, whose nickname was "Ducky," was a big part of our lives. He was close with my dad and my other pap. He stayed with us all the time.

The shift in energy took place when he got sick. I was six years old when I experienced the first devastating death in my life. I loved my pap. He was always taking care of me. I knew he was seriously ill, but I never thought he would die. I did not know what death was. I had never even lost a pet at that point in my life.

I remember it as though it was yesterday. My grandfather died on St. Patrick's Day. I *knew* he was gone. When I arrived home from school that day, my mom was standing at the kitchen sink, crying. I remember her holding a dinner plate in her hand and she was trembling.

She said, "I am still setting the table for him for dinner."

I just stood there waiting for her to tell me. Then she said that my pap went to heaven that day. I was sad because she was sad. I could feel her sorrow and pain. After losing my pap, things got harder for me.

This was when I started to feel fear and sorrow. I was connecting to spirit in a different way from how I had before that time. I was scared and confused and started having nightmares. Dark shadows of figures appeared in my house. I started sleepwalking too. Once I woke up standing in the middle of the basement in the dark. As I became fully awake, I realized I had been traveling in my sleep. I only recalled being with someone or looking for something.

We did not think much about the experience at the time. My mom said I appeared to be awake during these episodes.

How did I get down into the basement? There were no lights on as I walked down the steep steps, and it was pitch black. This weird experience happened more than a handful of times.

I was never alone. I always had spirits around me. They even stopped me from going out the front door a few times.

I recall many occasions when I woke up in the middle of sleepwalking. I would start laughing because I knew what I was doing. Other times I was told about what happened afterward. My mom said once I came out talking to her, crying, and saying, "I just want to go home."

It was a little freaky. While the sleepwalking did not go on for a long time, it happened often enough to etch itself on my memory. I wondered if I was being lured by someone or something while I slept—especially if I was going down into the basement. I did not always remember what happened.

I recall waking up not knowing where I was and running for the stairs. That happened so often I felt like I was living in the movie *Groundhog Day*. The same occurrence kept repeating over a short period. I was undergoing a big transition without my caregiver, my pap, whom I loved so dearly. When he died, I lost a big part of me and what I knew to be normal back then.

As my life as a psychic medium unfolded, part of my journey was revisiting the impressions and traumas of my younger days. The missing pieces to our life puzzles often can be found when we reexamine our past. Reexamining our experiences can link us to the answers we seek as adults. We then can better understand ourselves and learn how our experiences shaped us positively or negatively. My journey taught me how lower energies can influence us on the physical plane. But these experiences in childhood were only the beginning.

CHAPTER SEVEN

A Haunting

While buying your first house *is* a big step, I never thought that being a first-time home buyer at the age of 26 would help mold me into the person I would become. I was so excited to finally have my own home. I had no idea of the strange events that would unfold. The life-altering experiences I will share with you here happened over a five-year period.

When we did the initial walk through of the home, I saw an empty shell and thought it had great potential to fix up. The place had a strong energy that I felt drawn to. At that first viewing, we noticed the owners had positioned everything they owned on one floor of the two-story house, which seemed odd to me. Also, all their belongings resided in one space, the living room. I assumed that was because they were selling the place. However, now that I look back at what happened to my family and me, I can see they did this for an entirely different reason.

We got moved in and settled within a few days. I felt excited and happy. My kids were in grade school, and my youngest was beginning in the Head Start program that year, so I had some free time during the day to work on remodeling the house.

During this period, I also was taking care of my maternal grandfather who had stage four cancer. I was working in the healthcare field at the time as a certified nurse's aide and doing full-time restorative therapy, a process that involves helping patients improve mobility and function, which enhances outlook as well as physical wellness.

I have been a caregiver since I was a little girl. My mom had several health issues, and I helped her when she was sick. I gained a lot of informal medical education watching her go in and out of hospitals my whole life.

I would assist my grandfather at his home between my work shifts, but eventually we realized he needed full-time care, so I helped my parents get him into the skilled nursing facility where I worked. Having to make this move was difficult on everyone. My kids were used to visiting their pap at his home. Now they went on my days off to see him at the facility. I explained to them that Pappy was sick and needed more attention than I could give. I let them know the nurses would take care of him now. It was devastating for them not to be able to see him as much.

My job as a restorative therapist there was demanding and required a lot of paperwork and even more physical labor. Still, I loved my position. Helping people was and remains a passion for me. I felt blessed that I could work where my pap was living. You could say I was protective of him. My co-workers were amazing people, and he had some great nurses who were my friends.

At the time, I was what they call a floater, working different shifts. I did not have a set schedule and was constantly on call, so I was able to spend time on remodeling in my off hours when everyone else was out of the house.

Everything was slowly falling into place or so I thought. When I gutted most of the house, I came across black-and-white pictures of a family in the horsehair plaster. I discovered more photos in the upper loft of the detached garage. Some were of members of the family and some just random pictures. I realized the home was one of the first built in the town. The house next door, which was identical, had been constructed by the same person.

My house was over a hundred years old and surely had its own story to tell. My mom's first cousin and her husband were the previous owners. They lived there for several years. I honestly believed that since the previous residents were family members, the place was safe. But soon this new home would become my worst nightmare.

I had a lot going on while moving into a new home, working full time, and trying to take care of my family. Many major life changes seemed to be happening all at once.

I started to notice small occurrences at first. My animals began behaving strangely. It started with my dog growling at the foot of my bed. He would wake me at all hours of the night, snarling with this dead stare in his eyes. In the seven years I had him before this point, I had never heard or seen him do this.

Days after moving into the house, things started to change. I heard doors slamming when I was the only one at home. I would go upstairs and none of the doors would be shut. I left all of them open. It was cold out and all the windows were closed. I had to investigate every sound. My master bedroom closet door always seemed to open by itself although I kept shutting it tightly. All the doors were original to the house and made of heavy hardwoods.

The first few weeks I tried to explain away some of the noises. You begin to get familiar with the sounds of your new home. I am not the kind of person to jump to conclusions right away. I was only uncomfortable when my dog continued to growl at the foot of my bed. I was getting disturbed hearing this night after night.

I began having horrible dreams. The nightmares always focused on bad things happening to my family. I saw horrifying, vivid images of my children being abducted by strangers. In the dreams, my girls would be outside playing in our front yard as some man walked up to them. I watched this happen from inside the house. I saw the man reach for their hands, grab them, and march off with my baby girls as I stood there screaming and pounding on the glass of the window. They just kept walking away with him. I was mute in the dream. No sound came from me even though I was screaming as loudly as I could. It did not even matter. I could shout and pound and nobody would hear me.

I felt like I was in a box and had no control over the outcome of the nightmares. I remember the dreams were always in black and white—no color at all. I woke up shortly after that and felt relieved, excusing it as a *release dream*. We have these and they commonly relate to a deep-seated fear.

These experiences became more frequent and slowly got worse over time. I started to hear disembodied voices at all times of the day when no one else was home. I felt like I was being constantly watched in every room. Yes, even the bathroom. It was disturbing.

I kept my experiences to myself in the beginning. I really had no reason to tell my children about it since doing so would only scare them. When my kids started having major mood changes and behavioral issues, I got really concerned. A parent's job is to make sure our kids feel safe and are protected.

I have been developing and training actively as a psychic medium for many years. My intuition told me something was different about the experiences in this house. Something was off about the energy, and it was starting to affect my kids. My protective radar as a mom was on high alert at this point.

My children have always known from a young age that they could talk to me or ask me anything without being judged. I freely expressed all things spiritual to them, and I always taught my kids they could talk to me about *anything*. In our home, encouragement was given to speak up and share freely without facing judgment. I made sure that this was instilled in them.

Most of us never have the opportunity for such openness with our parents. I am so glad that I broke that pattern for my kiddos. I wanted to make sure to mentor and guide my own children about the spiritual realm—something I missed having when I was young. I never wanted them to feel they were misunderstood. I tried my best to listen and help them as they were growing up and to validate them when I could.

I am a spiritual person with sensitive, empathic children. I thought it would be easy to help them because I understood what they were going through and could help them remain open. I was wrong. We all have our own unique experiences and are affected in different ways. Trying to protect my children and keep them safe, naturally, I wanted to shield them from the monsters that I faced.

My children had been vocal about seeing deceased loved ones since they could talk. Every house we rented always had a spirit or two attached to it. I was used to this and even expected it. I knew how to cross them over if they needed help. We also could co-exist with spirits. Most times they are not earthbound and just love to visit. Only time would tell what I was dealing with in this new home.

The Apparition

In late September we planned a slumber party for my youngest daughter's birthday. We decided to have it on a Friday evening after the kids got home from school. I figured it would give them a chance to play outside until dark and wind down. They wanted pizza for dinner and planned on having a movie night. I had no idea that this evening would be the first of many disturbing encounters for my family.

The kids played outside until dark. Then I called them in to watch their movie. We had about seven girls including my two. They all went upstairs to pick out their sleeping spot before the movie started. When I came up the stairs a few minutes later, I found a few of the kids standing at the doorway of the bedroom.

As I was coming through the hall towards the bedroom, one of the girls looked behind me. She pointed past me and asked me, "Is the little girl behind you coming?" I was coming from downstairs and knew no other kids were behind me. I stood there looking at her, wondering what she was talking about.

I turned around to see if maybe someone did show up. No one was there, so I asked her who she was talking about.

She said, "I saw a little girl with pajamas on standing behind you." The child who'd glimpsed the girl behind me ran back into the bedroom with the other girls. When I came in, she asked me where the other little girl had gone.

I had to tell her that no one else was there. She froze for a second and said that my kids told her our house was haunted. This is how I found out they were hearing and seeing things too. I knew my kids would not let this incident pass at that point. Sleepovers and scary stories—Houston, we have a problem.

I was in shock that this spirit or whatever it was showed itself to the children. I was hoping the girls would forget about it. I did not want to have to call parents in the middle of the night and try to explain what had happened. Guess what followed? Of course, I had to call the parents for one of the girls.

They all went to sleep except for Emma, who was frightened and crying her little eyes out. She came into my bedroom, woke me, and asked me to call her mom. When I asked her what was wrong, she told me all the girls were telling scary stories. I knew it!

I tried to reassure Emma and explain to her that everything was okay. I took her to the kitchen to talk with her. This little girl was petrified and not calming down for me. I wished she would have talked to me about why she was so scared. Until this day I am not sure if she'd had a personal experience or not.

It was around 3:00 in the morning when her mom came to pick her up. The rest of the night was quiet. Everyone woke up for breakfast that morning and asked where Emma was. I let them know she'd left early in the morning. Emma never came back to our house after that night.

A full body apparition of the little girl was seen and heard several times after that. I talked with my daughters' friend who'd seen the specter. She told me the spirit looked a lot like my youngest daughter Tate. I felt creeped out about that. This was later validated by my children's father, who was a skeptic.

About six months after the first encounter, I was away for military training. I was gone over Easter weekend when I received a call from my husband. He phoned to wish me a happy Easter and told me about the experience he'd had the night before. He said that he was down in the kitchen getting a drink before going to bed. The whole downstairs was laid out in a circle; you could make a circuit from the living room to the kitchen to the dining room.

He said he noticed the cat, Oliver, was behaving strangely, standing up against the archway between the dining room and kitchen. It looked like the cat was getting ready to walk into the dining room until something spooked him—stopped him dead in his tracks. Oliver was acting frightened with his hair puffed up and standing on end. I was in shock to hear something like this coming from my husband's mouth.

The cat was reacting to a presence that went past him. It was the little girl. She was giggling when she stormed by my husband into the dining room. What made this even creepier was that my husband thought it was our daughter. He asked what she was doing up and told her to go to bed. Then he walked around the house but she was nowhere to be found.

When he was telling me what happened, I could tell he was concerned and unsure of what he had seen. He said that he knew she could not have gotten by via the stairs or even passed him without his noticing. So he went upstairs to see why she was playing games and not in bed. He went to check on Tate to see where she went. When he got to their bedroom, they both were fast asleep.

I felt certain he was freaking out. I am the believer in spirits, not him. There I was in Missouri, and there was nothing I could do but wonder if my kids were okay.

Earlier that morning in my barracks, I woke up feeling like something was watching me. I rolled over in my bunk and saw something staring me right in the face. I will not go into details because I do not like to talk about it. Just trust me when I say it looked like something out of the worst scary movie you ever watched.

This thing peering at me was small and sitting there just watching me. I jumped back almost falling out of the other side of the bunk. I knew something was going on at home. I could feel it. I knew in my gut that this was different from the spirits I typically encountered. This was serious and something was wrong. What confused me was that I never saw the little girl.

Whatever this was, it was playing games with us from the start. It took time for me to put all the pieces of the puzzle together. We heard weird noises, strange voices, and multiple voices at times. I could smell smoke in one room of the house every so often. The odor was always in my son's bedroom.

I was worried for us after the two incidents happened so close together. After I arrived home about a week and a half later, we were all doing great and the house was quiet. Not much happened for the next few days. But I had to leave again for another two weeks soon and felt apprehensive about being away.

Those few days I spent at home felt good. I needed to have some family time. On the third day of my next time away for training, I woke up and rolled out of my bunk with a migraine from hell. I went out to the shooting range until I could not stay any longer. By midday

I ended up at the hospital, getting Imitrex shots for my migraine.

I came in from a long day and crashed in my bunk to sleep off the medication. My phone rang. On the other end of the line, my daughter was telling me that the fire department was at the house. She said her dad did not want her to call me about it. He knew I would worry because I was away.

When I asked her what had happened, she said she woke up smelling smoke and screamed for her dad. Then she awakened her sister and brother to get them out of the house. I just stood in panic, thinking how bad that could have been if she did not wake up. I was pissed no one called me right away.

After I got off the call from my daughter, I phoned my husband to make sure everyone was okay and find out what damage was done to the house. He told me he knew I would only worry, being away from home. He said everyone was fine and there was nothing I could have done.

The house did not have much damage. I asked him what the fire department thought about how the fire started. Although my house was over 100 years old, all of the wiring had been redone in the '80s. They had no idea what could have caused the fire and said that they found nothing to explain how it started.

The fire began in my son's room between the walls. It was a mystery. I never considered the fact that I used to smell smoke only in his room.

I did not tie this to paranormal happenings. There was too much going on to connect the dots. All I knew was that my life was filled with far too many strange occurrences since we moved into that house.

I tend to be scientific and skeptical. Of course, when I see, feel, hear, or *know* something, I do not dismiss it. I am just down to earth and realistic. I have never questioned my gifts or how I receive information. At this point, my life felt scattered and I had that nagging feeling that something was *off*. I just could not put my finger on what was going on.

Things were happening all around us and not *to* us yet, or so I thought.

CHAPTER EIGHT

Where There Is Light, There Is Also Dark

Nothing is ever really as it seems. Over the previous 14 years, I had received a lot of informal training and had begun to learn how to fight against the negative and darker energies. This is when my life changed forever because my children were being targeted.

Every family goes through hard times. No one is perfect. I had my challenges with keeping the kids involved in after-school activities. My son played football and the girls played softball and basketball. At times, it was not easy trying to coordinate everyone's activities. We did our best to make all the schedules work.

While it was challenging, we were all trying to settle into our new home and get used to the new routines. We managed to get our lives in order, and everyone was taken care of. I felt at peace with our decisions and life seemed to be falling into place for us, or so I believed.

One day at work I got a call from my son's school. His teacher was concerned about the pictures he was drawing.

Art is one way for children to express themselves. It is normal for a child to draw their experiences and scenes from their lives. His teacher wanted to set up a meeting with my husband and me and suggested the school counselor attend. I had no idea what this was about.

From a Child's Perspective

We went into the meeting and sat down. The counselor was there with his teacher. She had his pictures laid out with a sentence on the back explaining what he drew about. I looked at the sketches and read the back of his work.

My son was drawing pictures of dead people. Since he knew I was about to leave for military duty, he expressed what he could not articulate about how he was experiencing that reality internally. He sensed the danger to me, his mom, and the potential for death to others.

I was not concerned about him drawing spirits, but the looks on the faces of his teacher and counselor told a different story. I sat in front of these people who were responsible for teaching my son and thought, *what now*? Here was yet another school situation with a teacher and counselor who saw the situation completely differently from me. I knew my son was born with this gift. Since he was a toddler and could talk, I also was aware he could see and hear spirits. He was my third child, and I had been through this with his sisters already.

The teacher and counselor felt something was wrong with him. I believed he was being judged. I had been through this my whole life.

"Why does he draw ghosts?" they asked.

I was being questioned about something they had never encountered. I was not prepared to explain any of this to them. I just sat and listened to what they had to say before I spoke. Their concern was that he was starting to show changes in his behavior during school. Their response to the drawings was to assume he was being influenced by TV or by his immediate family.

As long as he was not hurting anyone, I wasn't worried. His teacher said he was having a hard time focusing during class. She said he had to be redirected to keep on task and did not follow directions well. In my opinion, these issues should have been stated first. But I knew his pictures were the reason for the call.-

There was nothing I could say that would have changed how they saw the situation. I reassured them I would work with him at home, and we would talk to him about following directions. Inwardly, I was thinking, *here we go again*. His older sisters were spiritually gifted as well, so I knew the scenario all too well. Not everyone understands the ability for children to perceive what many others cannot.

We were dealing with a new home and new school, and it seemed like my children were constantly going to see the guidance counselor. I got several calls from the school and went to meetings to discuss how my kids expressed themselves. To the school staff, these were behavioral issues. I knew they had no clue what was going on. I made sure that if my children needed or wanted to talk to the staff they were welcomed to do so.

> There is a vast difference between traditional counselors, who interpret situations based on their "knowledge" or professional training alone, and intuitive counselors who use their intuition and spiritual gifts to help clients heal and transform from traumatic experiences. My personal experience as a mom experiencing how the traditional counselors viewed my kids stirred me to learn to work with children and families from a higher level of understanding and with great compassion.

No Coincidences

This house we bought to fix up and raise our kids in had more plans for us. While we had minor issues with the school noting changes in the behavior of all three of our kids, I did not link this to the house or see any reason to worry. I did not notice any patterns or behavioral changes at home with any of my kids. I was so busy working that I was blind to what was happening in my own home.

Over time the remodeling was slowly getting done, and I was not working 70 plus hours every week. Then I started to observe these changes in my kids. My son would not stay in his room to sleep. The kids were terrified of the dark.

Everything was getting weird. I noticed that all three of them had to have a radio or television on to go to sleep. I had to put night lights throughout the whole house. I could not keep my son from coming in and sleeping with me. This was not normal behavior for him. My son never crawled into bed with me.

Once when I was in a dead sleep, I heard my son scream at the top of his lungs. I bolted straight up, and he dove into my bed on top of me. He was hugging me so tightly and shaking with fear.

He said, "Mommy, that little girl is scaring me, and she will not leave me alone."

I held him and told him he would be okay and that he could sleep with me. About a minute after he got into bed with me, I heard a voice whisper into my ear, "Hello." This entity followed him to my room. I was not happy! This voice seemed to be taunting us. I was pissed. It is one thing to mess with me, but do not frighten my kids.

I jumped out of bed screaming at whatever was there to leave him alone. I was yelling and warning it to stay away. I said a prayer and put the white light around us for protection. Before this, I had never had any spirit follow or scare my kids. We never had problems at night.

My home became unstable and chaotic after that. We had already heard the voice of what sounded like a little girl. Several people had seen her, and we knew there were active spirits in our home. I was the most developed in terms of my gifts; yet I never saw the little girl. It was like this spirit was avoiding me at all costs.

Mischievous occurrences had been happening and my kids were now afraid. If you work with the light, what are the chances you also can attract the dark? I knew this was a big possibility. What was going on?

Moved Objects and Chaos

Everyone was having a hard time in the house. All of us were fighting and we could not sleep well anymore. My girls stayed in the same bedroom together to feel safe. I had three of us in my bed by the middle of the night on a regular basis. It was taking a toll on all of us. I started feeling threatened when I was home alone and often sensed I was being watched.

I went upstairs to clean when everyone was gone. I always felt like I wanted to run down those damn stairs after I finished up there. It was odd. One day I forgot the vacuum in Tate's room. When I ran back up to grab it, I heard something. It was one of those robot dogs going off on her bed. It scared the crap out of me. I'd just finished cleaning in that room and had put all her toys on the bed and the stuffed animals in the recliner to vacuum.

I seriously thought nothing of it and went over to shut it off. But when I turned the damn dog over, I got a frightening surprise: it was already off and had no batteries in it!

Although I was used to spirit antics, I was freaked out at this point. As I turned around to grab the vacuum, I saw my daughter's stuffed animals sitting in a perfect circle on the floor. I said, "Okay, not twice in one day!"

Screw the vacuum. I got the hell out of there. I was being toyed with. I had everything off that floor and those stuffed animals were on a recliner on the other side of the room. I did not like what was going on at all. Someone or something wanted my attention. I wanted answers.

I sat outside with my dog until I had to leave to pick the kids up from school that day. When you feel like you are not welcome in your own home, there is something wrong. I needed to get out of there. I'd spent too much time upstairs cleaning and was now literally being run out of my own home!

The Missing Purse and Negative Influence

The more time we stayed in the house, the worse it got for us. We had items go missing for days. My purse was lost for a week. Finally, we found it in Tate's bookbag. How it got there was the question.

Tate had homework every day of the week and her class folders were in her bag. I found my purse while putting her assignment folder back inside the bag. It just appeared there one morning. We had been getting things in and out of that bag all week. It made no sense.

Nothing was missing from my purse, and I wondered if one of my kids had hidden it from me as a prank. But they were as shocked as I was when I located it. Honestly, before finding it, I had been mad because I thought one of my kids had stolen the purse. The house was full of conflict. We were all fighting and blaming one another for the crazy havoc going on. We were stressed, not sleeping, and acting like we were against each other. My kids were not thieves, but I was questioning that.

We were about to get dealt another blow. The darker forces or negative entities know how to manipulate and trick us. We can be easily influenced by lower vibrations that manifest as depression or anxiety. The energies we sense or tune into can be from the living or the dead.

Becoming aware of energy shifts can help us recognize when something is not *right*. Unfortunately, I learned that the hard way. I got schooled by the best teachers, my kids. I started to see my oldest daughter distancing herself from me. I observed her attitude changing for the worse.

The calls from school told a story of her being defiant and not listening on a regular basis. She showed no interest in participating in the activities she had loved. My daughter had thrived in school and had valued a challenge. She was a part of the book club and read to other students throughout the week.

Now none of her actions matched who she was. The compassionate, loving child who cared about others had changed. My husband and I set up meetings to talk with her teachers and counselors to try to help her. I never had a hard time speaking with any of my kids before this, but she just shut down. I was concerned she was being influenced by her peers, but they were good kids. I knew their parents and the kids all grew up together. I never got a call when she stayed at their houses. I never had problems while she was home. I could not figure out what was going on with her.

Monsters Under the Bed

Sleep had been an issue for all of us since we moved into the house. I knew that much. I figured she was not sleeping enough, which turned her into a grouch at school. I had to find out what was causing this. I was upset and angry.

We had a talk about what was happening. My frustration deepened when I failed to get any straight answers. I took the extra light, her television, and radio out of her room. I had no idea that these were her comforts from the darkness and that they kept her safe. I grounded her from seeing friends and took away her privileges.

Having sensitives and insomniacs in the house at night is never quiet. When all the other houses on the street were dark and still, ours was lit in every room. Our home was always loud and busy. We used televisions and radios to drown out the noise from the spirits.

One night while I was downstairs in the kitchen, I heard what sounded like the radio on in my daughter's room. Her bedroom was at the top of the stairs above the kitchen. I stood there for a few seconds to see if she had her television or radio on. I had just grounded her and banned her from using either one.

I continued straightening up the kitchen for the night. As I was sweeping at the base of the stairs, I suddenly heard crying. I listened more intently to discover if she had the TV or radio on. I heard multiple voices coming from the top of the stairs, so I went up.

After I walked up the steps, I reached for the light switch around the corner. No television and no radio were on. I looked over to see my daughter under the covers. When I pulled the bedspread, blankets, and sheet down, I saw her violently trembling with tears streaming from her eyes. I asked her what was wrong.

She was clearly frightened. I asked her why I'd heard multiple voices coming from her room. She would not say anything. I sensed something in the room with us. I felt so bad for having taken away the things that made her feel safe.

I tried to get her to tell me what had happened. I knew what I heard, but I wanted her to talk to me and not shut down. I sat with her for a bit until she calmed down and we went downstairs to sleep on the couch.

This was why she was not sleeping. She was being interfered with and worn down by some not-so-nice spirits. I was mad! She had just moved into my old bedroom where our dog would sit at the foot of the bed and growl. We turned the dining room into a full bath and another bedroom. My girls' rooms were at opposite ends of the house now. They were separated.

The closet doors would open by themselves, and the dog was always growling at the foot of the bed. He was facing that door. Both of my girls' closets were connected. I was starting to connect the dots and see the patterns of where the activity was mostly taking place—upstairs and at the closet.

I could never sleep in that room. Now my oldest daughter was stuck in that same space. I never put two and two together. I was just hoping it was because of me and my gifts. I never would have let her take that room if I had known.

We had a big problem. Now that the kids had their own rooms, they were all targets. This began with just having a few small happenings as I call them, but it had escalated to spirits attempting to drain and harm my children. It all was making sense to me now.

The "monsters under the bed" had become a negative influence around my children. Their mental health began to suffer. My son and daughter were showing signs of depression and anxiety and having panic attacks. Our family was struggling with three deaths in the family all at once. My grandfather who lived in the nursing home, an aunt, and their great uncle had died in a short time span, which added grief to the mix of the madness.

With all these losses in three months on top of what was happening inside our house, I could not catch my breath. I felt like I was already defeated. I was stuck in this home where we were all being haunted. It felt like we all had a big bullseye painted on our foreheads. We were so sad and traumatized by all the recent events.

We all had disturbing experiences over a span of three to four years. I found out that all of us had similar stories. We all were seeing figures and hearing voices. At first it seemed innocent enough. The spirits hid and moved items in the house. Then they became physical and more threatening.

Twelve Years of Fighting

Two of us in the home were affected more than the others. I was still trying to figure things out. The nightmares—always related to my worst fears—continued for me over the years. In the dreams I was trying to get to my children to save them or help them.

I was physically attacked several times. When I tried to sleep, I heard noises coming towards me. I felt my arms and legs pinned down by some unseen force. I could not raise my head or scream. (This was not sleep paralysis.)

My oldest daughter and I were the main targets. I came to recognize that we were dealing with a dark entity. During the first few years, it disguised itself as the little girl. It hid from me and did not want to be known. This was uncommon. I had rarely seen or heard of people who battled something like this.

I am talking about a demon. I do not speak of this subject lightly. My family was torn apart, tormented, and it used us against each other. I moved out of the house thinking we would be safe and that we could go on. I was wrong. This darkness followed us for more than 12 years.

I attempted to save my family several times by getting traditional help through family and individual counseling. It never occurred to me to seek out spiritual help.

I thought the worst was behind us when I left that house in January of 2011 with only my clothes and my children. I had no idea that the most sinister circumstance had yet to play out.

I filed for a divorce a few months later and wanted to start over. By late March, I was working as an active duty recruiter and about to purchase a new home. I felt better once I was out of that house, but my kids still had to go back there to spend time with their dad. I was uncomfortable for them being at the house without me.

My kids had already taken a big hit with the separation of the family, which made the news of my deployment even more devastating. The perfect storm was brewing. We all went about our new schedules, and a few weeks went by with no new occurrences or issues. It seemed like things were working themselves out finally.

Attempted Suicide: A Parent's Worst Nightmare

The week came for the kids to visit their dad in the house. We rotated, each of us having custody every other week. It was hard enough for me having them away for a weekend, let alone the week they had to stay with their dad. It weighed on my heart. I had a feeling that something was wrong the night they left to go to their dad's.

I called the kids before bed to wish them goodnight and tell them I loved them. I'd just gotten off the phone when I had an intense sense that something was wrong. I did not know what, but I felt like I had to have my ex check in on the kids. I called and asked him to look in on our oldest daughter. It was around 10 o'clock on a school night.

I was on edge and felt sick to my stomach. I went into full-on anxiety and panic mode. I recognized my intuition was warning me. I got a call back saying all the kids were okay and they were in bed. What their father did not know was our daughter had taken a whole bottle of extra-strength Tylenol PM.

Later, a phone call awakened me. My daughter, scared and panicked, told me she had taken a full bottle of medicine. I raced over to pick her up and take her to the hospital, knowing I could get her there faster than calling for an ambulance since I was about two minutes away.

A parent's worst nightmare had become my reality. The emergency room needed to know the amount of the dose. The doctor and nurses had to call poison control to find out how to treat her properly. They ran labs and other blood tests to make sure she did not have liver damage. She was as white as a sheet and shaking from the poison in her system. After they stabilized her, they came to talk to me.

The doctor said she was lucky to be alive. I was so relieved and thankful. He said her blood test confirmed the amount she said she'd taken. He stated that if she lied about how much she'd taken they would not have been successful in reviving her. The doctor could not believe she survived. The medical staff could not figure out how she had no liver damage.

She was then transferred to the children's hospital 45 minutes away to recover. She slept for a few days. When she woke two days later, she was angry and crying. It had to be the saddest moment of my life, witnessing my first-born baby girl devastated that she had survived her suicide attempt.

Metaphysical or Mental

They brought in a psychiatrist to treat her for depression. He wanted to put her into a mental health facility to get continuous care and have treatment options. After a long discussion with him during which I expressed passionate disagreement, I signed off on taking full responsibility for her continued treatment after discharge. I would not allow her to be out of my sight and medicated by doctors who had no clue what had happened.

We had no warning signs. She shut down. Yes, she had severe depression and anxiety from being traumatized, from being haunted and hunted. Her will was broken down. There were times when I did not recognize my own child.

Some people consider this kind of thing a mental condition. The medical field identifies symptoms and puts them into specific categories. They label people bipolar, schizophrenic, or psychotic and treat them with medication. But we are spiritual beings, and our beliefs correspond to our experiences. I knew what we had all experienced living in that home.

It took a long time to identify what was going on in that house. It was different from any other haunting or paranormal experience we had encountered. We had several sensitives under one roof and a swinging open door that allowed entities to flow through our home. All the signs were there. An infestation was present that had lasted for years.

Watch for the Signs

Those signs were the shadowy figures, destruction of our family, unexplainable noises, and objects being moved. The attacks gradually became more physical. We were being tricked and manipulated. Over time we all felt broken down mentally, physically, and spiritually. We were targeted and oppressed by an entity that then attached to my child.

Although I later learned that I was the target for the demon, the means of getting to me was through my daughter. The entity took what I loved most and influenced her. This evil fed on what was most precious to me and tricked me to break my will. I saw my daughter become someone I did not know—a shell of the beautiful soul that once existed. I had not seen that person for years. You see, it needed an innocent to possess.

I fought for years to heal my child spiritually and traditionally. But nothing helped. Medication numbed her; mental hospitals destroyed her physical health. I saw my daughter go into what looked like psychosis. It started off with no sleep for almost a week. She could not eat or have the awareness necessary to eat. She was sleep deprived and starved. I could not hold a conversation that made sense with her anymore.

I watched for years as this evil tortured the child I loved. My daughter fought for her soul. She had lack of self-care, self-love, and self-worth. She vanished in front of my eyes. I felt helpless and defeated.

I was taking care of my father, who was battling stage four cancer, going back and forth with him to and from his appointments. In the midst of this, I was juggling visits to the mental hospital to see my daughter.

Her condition may have looked like serious mental health issues, but, in fact, this was the beginning of a partial possession, which appeared the same as full possession except that the evil entity would come and go. It could not take full possession of her body.

The darkness has nothing but time—time to plan, manipulate, influence, destroy, and finish what it set out to accomplish from the beginning. I hold a powerful light around myself. My children have a strong light around them. It waited for the perfect time for me to be completely broken.

Losing My Faith and Fighting for My Soul

A mother will do anything to protect and save her child. Anything. I challenged this entity and told whatever was taking hold of my daughter to come into me. To free the daughter I loved, I welcomed it in and allowed it to take me. My daughter has not had anything happen to her since that day. I was what it wanted the whole time. I just never knew it until then.

It could talk through her and influence her. It made her feel unworthy and helpless. I almost lost my child due to this force. It is real and this does happen.

After I took on this evil force, it took everything I ever cared about and made me feel nothing. I had no happy thoughts, no desire for the things I loved in my life. I could not care less.

I had all the signs and symptoms that my daughter had experienced. I felt like I was dreaming and could not wake up from this horrible nightmare. I felt numb—dead inside—with nothing but hate, anger, and hopelessness. I just wanted to die.

I could not say the Lord's prayer. I lost my faith, and I was in ruins over the death of my father. For 12 years I was targeted by evil. The last two I spent fighting for my soul and my life. I battled until I could not fight anymore. I had my last NDE (near death experience) in March 2019, which marked the end of that battle. I died.

Accepting Your Truth and Living Your Purpose

When I woke up from this experience, miraculously I could feel again. I wasn't numb anymore. I could feel my body again and my heart beating... and I could breathe.

I was given another chance at life! For several long years, I had been praying for a clear path to what I am here to do to be revealed.

Before that time, I had been so scared to be judged for just being me. I suffered greatly during the years that I hid all that I truly was. As I released my fear, the weight fell off of my shoulders. I finally felt it was safe to be who I am and to embrace my past, both the good with the bad, knowing it was all part of my journey of becoming who I am supposed to be.

By finally being able to accept myself as I am, a clear knowing that I had a mission, a calling to help others on a similar journey in my own special way, came flooding into my heart and soul.

I am extremely thankful for my family who stayed beside me during this experience. We fought together. Love is the ultimate form of salvation. Even in darkness the light still exists.

This is my truth and my story. I am now living my best life serving others and have the honor of working with the best in the paranormal field. As the owner of a global business as a spiritual healer, teacher, and mentor, I hold live events and travel to help and teach others.

CHAPTER NINE

Where to Go from Here

We are each unique and your journey may be considerably different from mine. But we all face life's challenges and sometimes feel lost or surrounded by shadows as we walk through the world. I have few regrets because I recognize that I signed up to learn some difficult lessons in order to evolve, but my biggest regret is not seeking the help I needed long ago. I fought by myself and never want anyone to feel alone in such circumstances. Know that there are resources to assist you in the form of nontraditional, experienced practitioners. I am in your corner to help you find the path to a better life, free of the shadow that may seem to engulf the world or your own life.

If you are facing similar challenges to those I encountered, I hope my story sheds some light and offers some insights and hope. The world of spirit contains far more than what is visible and measured by science. I have lived experiences that fall considerably outside the realm of traditional understanding. I am grateful to have come through all of it embracing the lessons I have learned.

In this book I've offered you insights to help you progress, evolve, and live your purpose and shared some of my own experiences to let you know that whatever you are going through, you are not alone. We write our stories every moment of every day based on our thoughts, emotions, and soul agreements. But even with those pre-incarnation contracts, we still have free will to explore how we will live the lessons of our souls. We decide whether to embrace the evolution our spirits seek to bring us or to fight against our higher self. We choose whether or not to sink into self-doubt, to play the role of victim, or to rise into our power and manifest our purpose and our dreams. Believe me, I know that can seem like an impossible mission sometimes. When we are in the middle of the struggle, it can be hard to see the way out. But that way exists, and my profound hope is that you will embrace the tools and insights shared between the covers of this book and also find other means along the way that will spark the inner knowing that you can succeed.

As someone who has experienced profound trauma, both physical and emotional, and more loss than I dreamed possible, I know how easy it is to get lost along the path and to feel depression and grief in its different stages. I also recognize that no one else can lift us out of that place of despair. Others can act as guides and helpers, but we have to break the cycle of limiting habits and beliefs. We have to imagine bigger and better and find within ourselves the strength and determination to discover our purpose, to live our light, to rise into our higher self.

In the pages of this book, I have shared with you many of my own struggles. I hope yours are much less intense and that you never have to face down the darkness as I have in order to evolve. But whatever your personal path may be, it is vital that you recognize in yourself the powerful spirit you are and align with that truth.

Stretch yourself beyond your comfort zone. If you catch yourself napping your way through life, either you choose to move beyond the routine, or the universe is likely to send something to shake you out of that state of stasis. Newton's first law says objects will stay at rest or in uniform motion *unless compelled to change by an external force*. As someone who has faced a lot of that "external force" in order to transform my life, I can say firsthand that it's much easier to just keep shifting toward your goals and growing into your purpose without the prompting of outer events. Complacency gets us nowhere. We have to keep moving.

Part of that evolution is diving into our own inner truths. No matter what you have been taught or how much negative programming you received as a child, you are up to the task of unearthing your personal beliefs, those that speak to your soul, and you are capable of letting go of those that restrict your progress. You also have the power to heal and release the deep-seated issues and patterns that have prevented you from living the life you dream of.

If I could wave a magic wand to help you, I would intend that you be able to easily identify your limiting patterns and thoughts, dig to your core for the answers to healing them, discover your purpose and goals that align with your deepest desires, fuel the thoughts of those desires with joy and love, believe in your vision and your ability to manifest it, and act accordingly. Of course, I'm not your fairy godmother, so I can only invite you to walk that path yourself—with the assistance of spirit guides and human mentors or coaches who can help you see what stands in your way and find the best means to navigate the path forward.

When you align with your soul and seek to live according to the wisdom of your higher self, you can bring miracles into this world and create the life you've envisioned. Honor your soul. Trust, believe, and receive so you may evolve and rise beyond the trials of your life. Our challenges can become our greatest teachers, enabling us to integrate the wisdom learned and to then share with others who walk a similar path.

> *"The day science begins to study the non-physical phenomena; it will make more progress in one whole decade than in all the previous centuries of its existence."*
>
> —Nikola Tesla

A Special Bonus Gift from Sky

Now that you've read ***Find Your Voice in the Darkness: Shine Your Light to Serve Your Soul Purpose,*** you are on your way to finding your true purpose that aligns your deepest desires and knowing how to manifest your vision and navigate your way forward, despite the darkness, grief, or pain you may have experienced before now.

In order to help you along the journey, I've created a special bonus gift just for you as a reader of this book. It's a ***Spiritual Journey Meditation*** kit, a series of three audio meditations to help you

- Reduce anxiety and connect with your natural state of being.
- Connect with your loved ones, spirit guides, and angels who help you during your journey.
- Explore how to ground yourself, clear your energy and recharge to open your natural gifts to serve your soul purpose.

Just go to www.MediumSkyRaye.com/freegift and tell me where to send it.

The sooner you know how to align with your soul and seek to live according to the wisdom of your higher self, the faster you can bring miracles into this world and create the life you've envisioned.

I'm in your corner. Let me know if I can help further.

Here's to your healing, peace, joy, and aligned purpose!

Best,
Sky Raye

Glossary

Astral: subtle body and plane of existence that coexists with and survives the death of the human body.

Astral Body: A body which exists outside the physical body as a vehicle for the soul or consciousness. It is understood as being of the emotional nature or emotional body.

Aura: Energy field emanating around a person or object. This is an outline of cascading color and held to represent soul vibrations and reflection of surrounding energy fields.

Channeling: Psychic channeling is a form of mediumship that transfers information from passed loved ones or guides through the medium.

Clair: From the French, this word literally means "clear" and is used to describe types of sensitivity corresponding with our physical and intuitive senses. Clair begins the words that express the types of intuitive abilities.

Claircognizance: Clear knowledge. This term relates to psychic knowledge without any physical explanation or reason. This type of intuition includes precognition or future knowledge and retro-cognition of the past.

Clairvoyance: Clear vision. This intuitive vision is the ability to see objects, actions, or events distant from the present without the use of one's physical eyes. Clairvoyance transcends time and space, and visions are mostly seen through the third eye (mind's eye).

Clairaudience: Intuitive auditory perception or hearing is the ability to experience sounds or words and extra-sensory noise from a spiritual or unseen source.

Clairsentience: Clear feeling. A person's ability to acquire intuitive knowledge by feeling through the body.

Clairsalience: Clear smelling. Intuitive smell also known as clairscent or clairscentency. This involves smelling fragrances or odors without the use of the physical nose.

Clairtangency: Intuitive knowing experienced by touching. This is also known as psychometry. The person handles objects or touches something and receives information about the object, its owner or history.

Collective Consciousness: The set of shared beliefs, ideas, and moral attitudes which operate as a unifying force within society.

Demon: In religion, folklore, and mythology, a demon is a supernatural being that has generally been described as a malevolent spirit.

Empath: Sensitive human beings who are able to intuitively experience the feelings of others. Because of their high sensitivity, empaths feel and often absorb other people's emotions or physical symptoms. There are many different types of empaths.

Entity: Something that has a distinct, separate existence.

Etheric Body: Life force body or aura that constitutes the "blueprint" of the physical body and sustains the physical body.

Etheric plane: The level of existence beyond the physical that contains the life-sustaining force of living beings and the vital energy in all-natural processes of the universe.

Ghost: A manifestation of a spirit or the soul of a dead person who has remained on Earth after physical death.

Higher Self: The eternal, conscious, and intelligent aspect of being. This term is used by multiple belief systems.

Intuition: An immediate form of knowledge that comes to the knower by a means other than reason, conscious experience, study, or intellect.

Law of Attraction: Every thought or emotion has a frequency that emits a signal and draws to you a matching energetic experience. Like attracts like.

Law of Cause and Effect: Every effect has a precise and foreseeable cause. Every choice or action has a definite and predictable outcome. All that we experience in life is the result of a specific cause.

Law of Correspondence: tells us that our outer world is nothing more than the reflection of our inner world. This is an extraordinary principle and states our current reality is a mirror of what is going on inside us.

Law of Vibration: Everything is energy. Everything we can see and can't see vibrates at a specific frequency.

Meditation: A practice that alters the brainwave state to a slower level. The typical waking state of beta brainwaves (13-30 hertz or cycles per second) is slowed to eight to 12 hertz during alpha state and moves down to four to seven cycles per second in theta brainwave state. Slowing the brainwaves allows for deeper levels of relaxation, stress reduction, and in some cases heightened spiritual or intuitive awareness. These states can be experienced through many forms of meditation including conscious breathing, focus on sounds (singing bowls, gong, music) or objects such as mandalas, guided visualization, meditation through movement or dance, and many other methods.

Medium: A person who possesses the ability to communicate with spirits of deceased people and pets.

About the Author

Born as Amy Caprio in central Pennsylvania, Sky Raye is a natural born Psychic Medium. She's a spiritual healer, teacher, psychic advisor, counselor, evidential medium and self-transformation coach. As a forensic psychic medium, she works with law enforcement on unsolved and missing persons cases. Donating time to help solve missing persons cases is one of the ways she gives back to her community.

Sky holds public and virtual events and is a public speaker, spiritual teacher, and an intuitive empathic healer. She can read energies of both the living and the dead. Sky's devotion to helping find answers to help explain and help others understand the unknown has always been a passion—something that started at the age of eight. Her other passion is helping inspire, motivate, and guide others on their soul purpose after trauma and loss.

Sky discovered her soul purpose through her years of work in behavioral and mental health, both her formal education and personal experiences with the paranormal, and her vast and diverse life experiences. Known for her fine-tuned skill set that she has developed over many years of her journey, Sky is devoted to helping others find answers and better understand the unknown. She works intuitively and energetically with her clients to provide results that are both realistic and tangible.

She helps clients connect to loved ones who have crossed over to the other side, bringing healing messages to provide solace to those living with grief. Through her connection with the other side, Sky shares her validations that our loved ones are very much at peace. Their spirits continue to stand beside us in our everyday lives. Knowing that everything is energy, she assures us that the soul continues living even more vibrantly after we shed the physical body.

Sky offers personal coaching to help clients identify and connect to their higher self so they can serve their soul's purpose. She works intuitively and holds a sacred space to help guide clients to self-identify past beliefs, negative programming, and unbalanced areas. Unresolved issues that may have stemmed from childhood trauma, generational habits passed down, and even past lives may have left us feeling empty or fearful or created blocks and thought processes that no longer serve our higher self.

Sky lives in rural Pennsylvania with her family, working from home, and traveling to serve her clients and students all over the world. She regularly participates in paranormal events and is available for your event both online and offline. To contact her for more information, visit her social media pages or her website (https://MediumSkyRaye.com)

www.ingramcontent.com/pod-product-compliance
Lightning Source LLC
Chambersburg PA
CBHW052101230426
43662CB00036B/1726